THE NATIONAL PARK COOKBOOK

By
Judy Giddings

Welcome to the National Parks

Bienvenue aux Parcs Nationaux

Bienvenidos a los Parques Nacionales

Wilkommen Zu Den National Parks

ようこそ、アメリカの国立公園へお越し下さいました。

Additional copies may be obtained by addressing:

National Park Cookbook, Park Press
201 San Mateo Drive
Hot Springs, AR 71913

$12.00 per copy plus $2.50 for postage & handling

Printed in the United States of America
TOOF COOKBOOK DIVISION

670 South Cooper Street
Memphis, TN 38104

ACKNOWLEDGEMENTS

A huge thanks goes to family and friends for contributing recipes. This author is forever grateful.

A special thank you to the following national parks for sharing their photographs: Carlsbad Caverns National Park, Cavern Supply Company, Colonial National Historical Park, Great Smoky Mountains National Park, Hot Springs National Park, Jefferson National Expansion Memorial, Mount Rushmore National Memorial, National Capital Parks, Shenandoah National Park, Statue of Liberty National Monument, Yellowstone National Park, Yosemite National Park.

Thank you Mike Booher for the use of your wonderful photographs of Cape Hatteras and Sugar-Sugar girl at Great Smoky Mountains.

To LouAnn Anderson, this author really appreciates your expertise in setting the book to print. Thank you.

To Lois Baker, thank you for contributing your artistic talent and graphic design expertise to the creation of the cover art.

Also, thanks to my special friends for their computer help, encouragement and continuing friendship.

Again, the project could not have been accomplished without the loving support of my dear family.

INTRODUCTION

This book has been a labor of love for the National Parks. Having been a part of the National Park Service family since 1964 has enabled my family to live and work in areas where most people dream to visit. The magnificent sights we've seen, the many friends we've made, and the experiences we've collected are for a lifetime of memories. I truly enjoyed a revisit to the parks through these recipes and history. I hope you enjoy _The National Park Cookbook_ and encourage you to visit a park as often as time allows.

Table of Contents

GRAND CANYON NATIONAL PARK

Grand Canyon National Park in northern Arizona is one of the world's outstanding natural wonders.

Most impressive is its immensity. Measured by the course of the Colorado River in the bottom, the canyon is 217 miles long and for most of this length, ranges from four to eighteen miles in width. The canyon averages one mile in depth. Standing on one of the canyon's rims, the South or North, one can scan the distant buttes, towers, and pinnacles sculpted by the elements of wind, water, temperature and time. The exhilarating experience is never to be forgotten.

The geologic features are as colorful as they are mysterious. Containing hundreds of shades of reds, browns, grays and greens, the canyon is almost a kaleidoscope as its colors change and shadows lengthen or shorten with each passing minute. Periods of sunrise and sunset are indescribable.

The canyon receives most of its visitation in the summer months but a visit anytime of year can be equally rewarding. To see it with a coat of winter snow, during a thunderstorm, or under a full moon only adds another mystical dimension.

Most visitors view the canyon from the South Rim but the North Rim offers an equally impressive view. It is about a four hour drive from the South Rim's Grand Canyon Village to the North Rim.

Hiking is a great way to explore the canyon's inner depths, but remember that such a hike is much like hiking a mountain in reverse. The last of the hike is climbing out, not walking down. Remember too, the temperature is about 25 degrees F warmer at the bottom. You must make advance preparations for a canyon hike.

The majesty of the canyon will almost take your breath away. It will also make you quickly say to yourself, "How was it created?"

THE GRAND CANYON

Abraham Lincoln Birthplace National Historic Site, KY offers an early 19th century log cabin, symbolic of the one in which Lincoln was born.

The sea and mountain meet at *Acadia National Park*, ME. Sporting a rugged coastline, a favorite for photographers, one can almost hear the sea splash against the granite coast.

Adams National Historic Site, ME is the home of father and son Presidents John Adams and John Quincy Adams who came from one of the leading families in American History.

Agate Fossil Beds National Monument, NE in western Nebraska features a collection of prehistoric mammal remains.

Allegheny Portage Railroad National Historic Site, PA tells the story of the first railroad crossing of the Allegheny Mountains. The railroad was built in 1831 and abandoned in 1857.

Lake Amistad at *Amistad National Recreation Area*, TX is an 85 mile long reservoir on the Rio Grande used by boaters and anglers.

Andersonville National Historic Site, GA commemorates a Civil War prisoner-of-war camp. During the 14 month existence of the Confederate camp, 45,000 Union soldiers were confined there and approximately 13,000 died.

Andrew Johnson National Historic Site, TN includes two of the president's homes and tailor shop. Johnson, who was also President Lincoln's vice-president, is buried in the national cemetery.

General Robert E. Lee invaded the North in 1862 at *Antietam National Battlefield*, MD. The battle, claimed to be the bloodiest of the Civil War, is considered a draw by most, but overall is viewed a Union moral victory.

There are 21 islands and 11 miles of Lake Superior shoreline accessible by boat at *Apostle Islands National Lakeshore*, WI.

General Robert E. Lee surrendered the Confederacy to Union Lt. General Ulysses S. Grant at *Appomattox Court House National Historical Park*, VA on April 9, 1865.

The giant arches are the products of erosion at *Arches National Park*, UT. Short hikes enable visitors to view the beauty and splendor of the arches, balanced rocks, towers and spires.

Arkansas Post National Memorial, AR was an ideal link for supplies going in and out of the Mississippi wilderness for the first French settlement.

Arlington House, The Robert E. Lee Memorial, VA is an imposing antebellum home of the Custis and Lee families located in Arlington National Cemetery.

CAPE HATTERAS NATIONAL SEASHORE

Assateague Island National Seashore, MD is especially interesting with beaches, migratory waterfowl and wild ponies.

It is fascinating to see a completely restored Great Kiva at *Aztec Ruins National Monument*, NM.

Bighorn sheep, deer, antelope, swift fox, bison and prairie grasslands make up the *Badlands National Park*, SD.

There are remarkable cliff house ruins of 13th century Pueblo Indians at *Bandelier National Monument*, NM.

Reconstructed *Bent's Old Fort National Historic Site*, CO was an Indian trading center on the Santa Fe Trail.

Big Bend National Park, TX has the exciting wonder of mountains and desert within the great bend of the Rio Grande.

Big Cypress National Preserve, FL provides a freshwater supply crucial to the Everglades National Park's survival.

Nez Perce Indians and the U.S. Army fought at *Big Hole National Battlefield*, MT in 1877.

Bighorn Canyon National Recreation Area, MT, formed by Yellowtail Dam, features 70 mile long Bighorn Lake, superb for fishing and boating.

Big Thicket National Preserve, TX has been called "the biological crossroads of North America," the point of eight separate ecological systems.

Just 21 miles east of Everglades National Park, *Biscayne National Park*, FL was created to protect the mangrove shoreline, coral reefs, and Biscayne Bay's flora and fauna.

A dark, sheer-walled canyon, *Black Canyon of the Gunnison National Monument*, CO is a twelve mile stretch of the deepest and darkest part of the Gunnison River.

The *Blue Ridge Parkway*, NC was designed to link the Great Smoky Mountains and Shenandoah National Parks. The 469 miles of roadway follow the crest of the Blue Ridge Mountains and give insight to the beautiful hill country.

Booker T. Washington National Monument, VA is the birthplace and early boyhood home of the famous black leader and educator.

Boston National Historical Park, MA boasts Bunker Hill, Old North Church, Paul Revere House, Faneuil Hall, Old State House and a portion of the Charlestown Navy Yard. One can almost hear "The British Are Coming," an echo of the past.

Appetizers & Beverages

GOLDEN GATE ARTICHOKE DIP

2 cans artichoke hearts, drained,
   diced
2 cups Mozzarella cheese, grated
1 cup mayonnaise
1 clove garlic, minced
1 cup Parmesan cheese, grated

Combine all ingredients and bake at
350 degrees for 35 minutes.

BROCCOLI DIP

1 10 ounce package broccoli,
   cooked, drained
1 small onion, chopped
¾ cup celery, finely chopped
1 tablespoon butter
1 8-ounce package garlic cheese
   spread
1 can cream of mushroom soup,
   undiluted
Dash of hot pepper sauce, paprika,
   cayenne pepper and
   Worcestershire sauce

Saute' onion and celery in butter until
tender. Chop broccoli in small pieces.
Add to onion mixture along with cheese
spread, soup and seasonings. Cook and
stir over low heat until cheese melts.
Serve warm with vegetables or corn
chips.
Yield: 4 cups

REDWOODS ARTICHOKE DIP

1 16-ounce carton sour cream
1 can artichoke hearts, drained and
   diced
3 tablespoons creamy Italian
   dressing
1 teaspoon Worcestershire sauce

Mix all ingredients together and serve
with vegetables or crackers.

ITALIAN VEGETABLE DIP

1   cup mayonnaise
1   cup sour cream
1   envelope Italian salad dressing
¼   cup green pepper, finely chopped
¼   cup red pepper, finely chopped

Mix mayonnaise, sour cream and salad dressing mix. Stir in red and green pepper. Refrigerate.

FT. LARNED DILL DIP

1   cup sour cream
1   cup mayonnaise
1   tablespoon parsley flakes
1   teaspoon dill weed
¼   teaspoon Worcestershire sauce
½   teaspoon garlic powder
½   teaspoon seasoned salt
2   drops hot sauce
Dash onion salt

Mix all ingredients together. Cover and refrigerate.

ACADIA SEAFOOD DIP

1   cup flaked crabmeat or imitation
½   cup Cheddar cheese, shredded
¼   cup cream cheese, softened
¼   cup mayonnaise
¼   cup sour cream
¼   cup Parmesan cheese, grated
¼   cup green onions, sliced
1   teaspoon lemon juice
¼   teaspoon Worcestershire sauce
⅛   teaspoon garlic powder
¼   cup bread crumbs

Mix first 10 ingredients together until smooth. Spread in a pie plate. Sprinkle with bread crumbs. Cover and bake at 350 degrees for 20 minutes or until bubbly. Uncover and bake 5 minutes more. Serve with crackers or vegetables. Serves: 6

CARLSBAD CAVERNS TAMALE DIP

1 large can tamales
1 can chili, no beans
3 tablespoons Worcestershire sauce
1 pound Velveeta cheese

Mash and mix tamales with chili and Worcestershire sauce. Cut Velveeta in small pieces; mix and heat.

LAVA BEDS SPINACH DIP

2 8-ounce packages frozen chopped spinach
1 16-ounce carton sour cream
1 16-ounce jar mayonnaise
1 package vegetable soup mix
3 green onions, chopped
1 4-ounce can water chestnuts, chopped

Cook spinach and squeeze out excess water. Mix sour cream, mayonnaise, soup mix, water chestnuts and onion with spinach. Serve chilled with crackers.

VOYAGEURS CHEDDAR WHEEL

1 pound sharp Cheddar cheese, grated
¾ cup mayonnaise
1 medium onion, finely chopped
1 garlic clove, minced
½ teaspoon Tabasco sauce
1 cup pecans, chopped
1 cup strawberry preserves

Combine all ingredients except strawberry preserves. Mix well. Put in ring mold. Chill. Unmold and place preserves in center. Or place in pie plate an spread preserves over top. Serve with crackers.

TUMACACORI CAVIAR

2   4-ounce cans ripe olives, chopped
2   4-ounce cans green chiles, chopped
2   tomatoes, peeled and chopped
3   green onions, chopped
2   garlic cloves, chopped
3   teaspoons olive oil
2   teaspoons red wine vinegar
1   teaspoon pepper
Dash of seasoning salt

Combine all ingredients and chill overnight.

HOT CRAB SPREAD

1   8-ounce package cream cheese, softened
2   tablespoons onion, grated
1   teaspoon horseradish
1   teaspoon lemon juice
Dash Worcestershire sauce
Salt, pepper, cayenne pepper to taste
¼   cup milk
1   7-ounce can crabmeat, drained and shredded
½   cup slivered almonds, toasted

Combine all ingredients, except crabmeat and almonds. Mix well. Fold in crabmeat, spoon into baking dish. Sprinkle almonds on top. Bake at 375 degrees for 20 minutes, or until bubbly. Serve hot with crackers.

LOUISIANA SHRIMP SPREAD

1   8-ounce package cream cheese
1   jar shrimp cocktail sauce
1   can shrimp, drained and chopped

Place cream cheese on serving dish. Layer shrimp and shrimp sauce over cream cheese. Two layers each. Serve with crackers.

ALASKA SALMON BALL

1 pound can salmon, drained
1 8-ounce package cream cheese
1 tablespoon lemon juice
2 teaspoons onion, grated
1 teaspoon horseradish
¼ teaspoon liquid smoke
Salt to taste
½ cup pecans, chopped
2 teaspoons parsley

Mix first 7 ingredients together with beater. Chill for several hours. Shape into roll. Roll in pecans and parsley. Chill overnight.

SHENANDOAH SAUSAGE BALLS

3 cups Bisquick mix
1 8-ounce package shredded Cheddar cheese
1 pound hot sausage

Microwave cheese slightly to soften. Knead all ingredients together. Roll into small balls and place on cookie sheet sprayed with cooking spray. Bake 350 degrees for 20-25 minutes.

EL MORRO TORTILLA PINWHEELS

1 8-ounce carton sour cream
1 8-ounce package cream cheese, softened
1 4-ounce can diced green chilies, drained
1 4-ounce can black olives, chopped and drained
1 cup Cheddar cheese, grated
½ cup green onions, chopped
Seasoned salt to taste
5 10-inch flour tortillas

Mix filling ingredients together thoroughly. Divide mixture and spread evenly over tortillas and roll up. Cover tightly with plastic wrap, twisting ends. Refrigerate several hours. Unwrap and cut into ½-inch slices. Electric knife works best. Serve with salsa.
Yield: 48

MANASSAS CRAB DELIGHTS

1   stick butter
1   jar Old English cheese spread
1½ teaspoons mayonnaise
½   teaspoon garlic salt
½   teaspoon seasoned salt
1   can crab meat
6   English muffins

Soften butter and cheese to room temperature. Mix with mayonnaise, garlic and salt. Add crab meat. Spread on halves of muffins. Freeze until solid, then cut each half muffin into pie shaped wedges. Heat under broiler until bubbly. Makes 96.

FRUIT CHEESE LOG

½   cup dried apricots
1   cup water
1   pound Monterey Jack cheese, shredded
1   8-ounce package cream cheese, softened
⅓   cup milk
1   teaspoon poppy seed
½   teaspoon seasoned salt
⅓   cup golden seedless raisins
¼   cup pitted dates, snipped
¾   cup walnuts, chopped

Soak apricots in water two hours; drain and chop. Blend cheeses. Add milk (or substitute sherry for milk), poppy seed and salt; mix well. Fold in fruit, mix well. Turn out on foil; make into log shape. Wrap securely in foil; chill until firm. Roll in nuts before serving. Serve with crackers.

TACO CHICKEN WINGS

½   cup all purpose flour
1   envelope taco seasoning mix
3   pounds chicken wings, tips removed and cut at joints (32 pieces)
6   tablespoons butter
1   cup crushed corn chips

In paper or plastic bag combine flour and taco seasoning mix. Add 2 or 3 chicken pieces at a time; shake to coat. Melt butter in 15x10x1-inch baking pan. Place chicken in pan, turning once to butter surfaces; then roll in corn chips and return to pan. Bake at 350 degrees for 40-45 minutes. Makes 32 appetizers.

CASA GRANDE NACHO PLATTER

1   pound ground beef
1½ tablespoons chili powder
½   teaspoon cumin
1   16-ounce can refried beans
1   4-ounce can chopped green chiles
1½ cups shredded Monterey Jack
      cheese
1½ cups shredded sharp Cheddar
      cheese
1   cup taco sauce
½   cup green onions, chopped
1   4-ounce can chopped black olives
1   6-ounce can frozen guacamole
      (or fresh)
1   cup sour cream
1   large bag tortilla chips

Brown ground beef and drain. Season with chili powder and cumin. Spread refried beans in a shallow 10-inch greased dish. Sprinkle on beef, followed by green chiles, Monterey Jack cheese and Cheddar cheese. Pour taco sauce over cheese. Bake for 20-25 minutes in a 400 degree oven. Garnish immediately with layers of green onion, black olives, guacamole and sour cream. Place dish on a platter and surround with tortilla chips. Serve warm. Serves: 12

GUACAMOLE-SHRIMP

½   pound shrimp, cooked and
      deveined
2   medium avocados, peeled and
      sliced
2   canned chili peppers
1   small onion, thinly sliced
1   garlic clove, minced
1   medium tomato, peeled and
      chopped
2   tablespoons lemon juice
1   teaspoon salt
1   tablespoon oil

Combine all ingredients, except shrimp, blending until smooth. Chop shrimp, add to ingredients, keeping a few for garnish. Yield: 2 cups

LONGFELLOW MUSHROOM CAPS

8   large mushrooms
1   package frozen crab cakes
2   tablespoons butter

Wash mushrooms; remove and save stems. Thaw 2 crab cakes to use for filling and place a tablespoon of filling into each mushroom cap. Dot with butter and bake in 350 degree oven for 15 minutes.

IOWA MICROWAVE CARAMEL CORN

4   quarts popped corn
1   cup brown sugar
¼   cup white Karo syrup
½   cup margarine
½   teaspoon salt
½   teaspoon soda

Place popped corn in brown paper bag. Mix brown sugar, syrup, margarine and salt and microwave on high for five minutes. Stir in ½ teaspoon soda and pour over corn in bag. Fold down bag, put in microwave for 1½ minutes, take out, shake and put in microwave for 1 minute. Shake again, microwave for 45 seconds then shake and microwave for 35 seconds. Shake and pour onto cookie sheet and separate. Cool.

FLORIDA FRUIT DIP

¾   cup brown sugar
¼   cup white sugar
1   8-ounce package cream cheese

Mix sugars with softened cream cheese. A great dip for a variety of fruits

CUMBERLAND ISLAND CRUNCH PUNCH

3 small packages gelatin
9 cups boiling water
4 cups sugar
4 cups warm water
1 16-ounce bottle lemon juice
2 46-ounce cans pineapple juice
3 quarts gingerale

Dissolve gelatin in 9 cups boiling water. Set aside. (Use mixture of flavors for color of punch wanted.) Blend sugar and warm water; bring to boil. Add syrup mixture to dissolved gelatin water. Let cool about 2 hours. Then add juices. Mix well. Pour into containers and freeze. Take from freezer about 3-4 hours before serving. Pour gingerale over punch just before serving. Recipe can be cut to ⅓ or ⅔. Punch is icy - no need to use an ice ring.

COFFEE POT PUNCH

1½ quarts cranberry juice
2 quarts apple juice
½ cup brown sugar
½ teaspoon salt
4 cinnamon sticks
1½ teaspoons ground cloves

Pour juices into 30 cup percolator. Place sugar and spices in basket. Perk as you would for coffee.

BIG CYPRESS ORANGE REFRESHER

1 6-ounce can frozen orange juice, thawed
⅓ cup dry milk powder
⅓ cup sugar
2 teaspoons vanilla
¾ cup cold water
10 ice cubes

Combine first five ingredients in a blender and process at high speed. Add ice cubes, a few at a time, blending until slushy. Serve immediately. Serves: 4

JOSHUA TREE PUNCH

1 12-ounce can frozen orange juice concentrate
3 12-ounce cans water
1 46-ounce can pineapple juice
1 6-ounce can frozen lemonade concentrate
1 quart ginger ale

Mix orange juice with water. Add remaining ingredients except ginger ale. Chill and serve. Add ginger ale just before serving. Makes 20 servings.

YELLOWSTONE NATIONAL PARK

Established in 1872 as the first national park in the United States, Yellowstone National Park is world renown. Situated in the north-west corner of Wyoming, the two million acre park contains geysers, hot springs, and hot bubbly pools amidst a wildlife sanctuary. Numerous mountains, rivers, streams and lakes complete its significant scenic panoramas.

One of the most notable features is Old Faithful Geyser. As its name implies, it erupts almost as regular as clockwork--about every 70 minutes with its plume approaching 175 feet high. It is one of 10,000 geothermal features in this wonderland of nature.

Wildlife is abundant and bison, elk, moose, deer, mountain sheep and bear can readily be observed. It is important to remember, however, that these animals are wild and even though some have grown accustomed to man in their environment, all should be observed from a safe distance. Numerous kinds of waterfowl and other birds, some rare or endangered, can be found around the fish-laden lakes or streams. Hunting or molesting wildlife is prohibited. Fishing may be permitted, but check first with the park staff for regulations.

Yellowstone cannot be seen in a day or two, and once within its boundary, you will easily determine why this beautiful land was chosen to lead the way for all national parks to be established as part of our American Heritage.

OLD FAITHFUL GEYSER

Sensational color contrasts are found in the pinnacles, walls and spires of *Bryce Canyon National Park*, UT.

The Buffalo National River, AR is a free flowing river that is both swift-running and quiet in stretches. It is a favorite of canoers.

Cabrillo National Monument, CA, named for a Portuguese explorer who claimed the California coast for Spain in 1542, maintains a whale overlook for visitors to see the migrating mammals.

Canaveral National Seashore, FL boasts the Kennedy Space Center, natural beach, wildlife and many species of birds.

Canyon de Chelly National Monument, NM with Indian ruins dating back to 350 A.D., is still regarded as a sacred place by the Navajo Nation.

Prehistoric Indian ruins and rock art are special features in the magnificent redrock landscape of *Canyonlands National Park*, UT.

Marconi's Wireless Station Site, ocean beaches, dunes and woodlands are impressive sights at *Cape Cod National Seashore*, MA. A solitary beach stroll or a trip to nearby Hyannis Port or Provincetown is a treat for all ages.

Families love to venture to *Cape Hatteras National Seashore*, NC for a beach vacation. The park was the first national seashore.

Fifty-five miles along the lower Outer Banks of *Cape Lookout National Seashore*, NC, are wonderful beaches and a memorable lighthouse.

A 25 mile Scenic Drive at *Capitol Reef National Park*, UT, enables visitors to view a combined wild and graceful national park. This park's raw beauty reminded early pioneers of an ocean reef.

In northeast New Mexico, breaking the prairie skyline, is the dormant volcano of *Capulin Volcano National Monument*, NM.

Carl Sandburg Home National Historic Site, NC contains Connemara, which was the farm home of the poet-author for the last 22 years of his life.

The Jimmy Carter National Historic Site, GA includes President Carter's residence, boyhood home and high school. The park's visitor center, which was the president's 1976 campaign headquarters, is in the railroad depot.

Casa Grande Ruins National Monument, AZ holds notable and unique four-story Hohokam Indian archaeological ruins.

Visit *Carlsbad Caverns National Park*, NM, tour one of the world's largest underground chambers and watch the bats fly at sunset for a fulfilling day.

COLONIAL NATIONAL HISTORICAL PARK

Castillo de San Marcos National Monument, FL is the oldest masonry fort in the continental United States.

Catoctin Mountain Park, MD has sparkling streams and cool mountain air surrounding the presidential retreat, Camp David.

Chaco Culture National Historical Park, NM interprets the Anasazi culture and allows exploration of the ancient expansive ruins.

Five islands off the coast of southern California make up *Channel Islands National Park,* CA. Sea lion rookeries, nesting sea birds and special island plants can be found on the islands.

The Chesapeake and Ohio Canal National Historical Park, MD is a 184 mile canal along the Potomac River between Washington, D.C. and Cumberland, MD.

The first national military park, *Chickamauga and Chattanooga National Military Park,* GA is site of a major Confederate victory in September 1863.

Chickasaw National Recreation Area, OK was named to honor the Chickasaw Indian Nation, former occupants of this land of rolling hills and springs.

Chiricahua National Monument, NM, once Chiricahua Apache territory, was a dude ranch, then a national monument.

The 38 room home of *Clara Barton National Historic Site,* MD was the headquarters of the American Red Cross for seven years.

Colonial National Historical Park, VA includes Jamestown Island, site of the first English settlement, Yorktown, scene of the final battle of the American Revolution and Cape Henry, landing site of Jamestown's colonists in 1607.

Colorado National Monument, CO is an example of wind, water, and time forming sheer-walled canyons and strange rock formations.

Crater Lake National Park, OR has the 1,932 feet deep Crater Lake, the deepest lake in the United States. It sits in the caldera of a volcano that erupted 7,700 years ago.

Craters of the Moon National Monument, ID offers splattered, molded, 2,100 year old lava flows and desert wilderness wildflowers all in one trip.

Cumberland Gap National Historical Park, KY is a mountain pass explored by Daniel Boone.

The preserved rural *Cuyahoga Valley National Recreation Area,* OH links the urban areas of Cleveland and Akron, Ohio.

Blue Mesa Lake in *Curecanti National Recreation Area,* CO, when full, is the largest lake in Colorado.

Salads

OREGON CAVES CHERRY SALAD

1   can pitted black cherries
1   13-ounce can pineapple tidbits
1   8-ounce package cream cheese, softened
¼   cup mayonnaise
1   3-ounce package cherry gelatin
1   3-ounce package strawberry gelatin
1   cup boiling water
7   ounces Coca Cola
1   cup nuts, chopped

Drain cherries and pineapple, set juice aside. Combine syrup from fruits to make 1½ cups reserve. Beat cheese and mayonnaise until smooth. Dissolve gelatins in water, cool slightly. Add syrup and cola. Chill until thickened. Fold in cherries, pineapple and nuts. Pour into mold. Serves: 12

HOOVER RASPBERRY SALAD

1½   cups boiling water
2   packages raspberry gelatin
2   packages frozen raspberries
1   10-ounce can crushed pineapple, with juice
½   cup pecans, chopped
1   cup sour cream

Add boiling water to gelatin; add raspberries immediately. Mix gently until thawed. Chill until slightly thick. Add crushed pineapple, pineapple juice and nuts. Place ½ mixture in 9-inch pan. Chill slightly. Fold sour cream into other ½ mixture. Pour carefully over top of chilled mixture. Chill until set.

SANDBURG LAYERED SALAD

1   cup red cinnamon candy
1   cup water
1   3-ounce package lemon gelatin
1½   cups unsweetened applesauce
2   3-ounce packages cream cheese, softened
Cream
Dash salt
½   cup nuts, chopped

Boil red candy and water slowly. Pour mixture over gelatin. Add applesauce. Put half mixture in mold. Cool well. Take cream cheese and add enough cream to make spreadable; add salt and nuts. When first half of gelatin is set, spread cheese mixture on top; pour on remaining cooled gelatin. Refrigerate to set. Serve with mayonnaise. Serves: 8

ELLIS ISLAND CRANBERRY SALAD

1   package cherry gelatin
1   cup hot water
1   cup celery, chopped
1   cup sour cream
1   can whole cranberry sauce
½   cup nuts, chopped

Dissolve gelatin in hot water. Cool. Stir in cranberries, sour cream and remaining ingredients. Put in serving bowl and chill until set.

PECOS FRUIT SALAD

½   cup mayonnaise
½   cup heavy cream, whipped
1   tablespoon lemon juice
2   cups peach slices, drained
1   cup miniature marshmallows
½   cup halved marachino cherries
1   banana, sliced
¼   cup nuts, chopped

Combine mayonnaise, whipped cream and lemon juice. Mix until well blended. Fold in rest of ingredients; chill. Serve on lettuce leaves. Serves: 8

CRATER LAKE DESSERT SALAD

1   can cherry pie filling
1   no. 2 can pineapple chunks, drained
3   cups miniature marshmallows
1   9-ounce carton cool whip

Gently fold together all ingredients. Refrigerate overnight. Serves: 12

LAKE MEAD MUSHROOM SALAD

2½ quarts water
3 tablespoons lemon juice
3 pounds small fresh mushrooms
2 carrots, sliced
2 celery stalks, sliced
½ medium green pepper, chopped
1 small onion, chopped
1 tablespoon parsley, minced
½ cup stuffed olives, sliced
1 2.3-ounce can ripe olives, sliced
Dressing:
½ cup Italian salad dressing
½ cup red wine vinegar
1 garlic clove, minced
½ teaspoon dried oregano
½ teaspoon salt

In large saucepan, bring water and lemon juice to a boil. Add mushrooms and cook 3 minutes, stirring occasionally. Drain; cool. Place next 7 ingredients in a large bowl. Combine all dressing ingredients in tight fitting jar; shake. Pour over salad. Cover and chill overnight. Serves: 8

BADLANDS SLAW

1 large head cabbage
½ cup red onion rings
1 cup oil
1 cup vinegar
1 cup sugar
1 teaspoon salt
1 teaspoon pepper
1 teaspoon celery seed

Chop vegetables, mix together. Chill. Remove some liquid before serving.

BIG BEND POTATO SALAD

6 large potatoes, boiled, peeled, and diced
4 celery ribs, diced
3 medium dill pickles, chopped
1 4-ounce jar diced pimientos, drained
3 hard-cooked eggs, diced
1 green pepper, chopped
¼ cup mayonnaise
1 teaspoon prepared mustard
1 teaspoon salt
Paprika

In a large bowl, combine potatoes, celery, pickles, pimientos, eggs and green pepper. In a small bowl, combine mayonnaise, mustard and salt; add to potato mixture and mix well. Put in serving bowl and sprinkle with paprika. Serves: 8

27

PADRE ISLAND SLAW

1½ pounds cabbage, shredded
1 teaspoon salt
⅔ cup sugar
⅓ cup cider vinegar
1 cup whipping cream
(do not whip)

Place shredded cabbage in covered dish in refrigerator for several hours. Mix ingredients in order given 30 minutes before serving. Chill and serve.

LASSEN MARINATED SALAD

1 head lettuce
1 cucumber, sliced
1 celery stalk, sliced
1 cup green beans, cut
2 carrots, shredded
1 cup cauliflower, broken pieces
⅛ teaspoon pepper
¼ cup oil
½ cup vinegar
⅔ cup sugar
¼ teaspoon salt
Dash garlic salt
Thousand Island dressing
Paprika
Bacon bits
4 green onions, chopped

Combine vegetables; marinate overnight in mixture of pepper, vinegar, oil, salt, sugar and garlic salt. Remove vegetables from marinade. Add broken-up lettuce. Toss vegetables and lettuce, add salt and pepper to taste. Place in individual bowls. Pour dressing over salad; sprinkle with bacon bits, dust with paprika.

SOUR CREAM CUCUMBERS

2 large cucumbers, peeled, sliced
1 large sweet onion, sliced rings
¾ cup sour cream
3 tablespoons vinegar
2 tablespoons sugar
Salt and pepper to taste

In a bowl, combine the cucumbers and onion. Mix remaining ingredients together and pour over cucumbers. Mix well. Chill. Serves: 8

GRAND TETON BEAN SALAD

2   cans pinto beans, rinsed
1   medium onion, chopped
1   medium green pepper, diced
1   medium sweet red pepper, diced
1   17-ounce can whole kernel corn,
    drained
DRESSING:
¼   cup ketchup
¼   cup vinegar
¼   cup olive oil
3   tablespoons brown sugar
1   tablespoon Worcestershire sauce
1   tablespoon chili powder
5   teaspoons Dijon mustard
1   teaspoon ground cumin
1   teaspoon salt
¼   teaspoon pepper

Place beans in large bowl. Add onion, peppers and corn; toss. In saucepan combine all dressing ingredients; simmer 10 minutes. Pour over vegetables and mix well. Cover and chill. Serves: 20

GATEWAY TOMATO SLICES

1   cup oil
⅓   cup vinegar
¼   cup parsley, minced
3   tablespoons, minced or 1 table-
    spoon dried basil
1   tablespoon sugar
1   teaspoon salt
½   teaspoon pepper
½   teaspoon dry mustard
½   teaspoon garlic powder
1   medium onion, sliced thin
6   large tomatoes, sliced thin

Mix first nine ingredients in a tight fitting jar. Layer onion and tomatoes in shallow dish. Pour marinade over; cover and chill. Serves: 12

MAMMOTH CAVE CORN SALAD

2   cups sweet corn
¾   cup tomato, chopped
½   cup green pepper, chopped
½   cup celery, chopped
¼   cup onion, chopped
¼   cup Ranch salad dressing

Combine vegetables in large bowl; stir in dressing. Cover and refrigerate until ready to serve. Serves: 8

SANTA MONICA COBB SALAD

½ head iceberg lettuce
½ bunch watercress
1 small bunch curly endive
½ head romaine lettuce
2 tablespoons minced chives
2 medium tomatoes, peeled, seeded and diced
1 whole chicken breast, cooked, boned, skinned and diced
6 slices bacon, cooked and diced
1 avocado, peeled and diced
3 hard-cooked eggs, peeled and diced
⅓ cup Roquefort cheese, crumbled
French Dressing (recipe follows)

Chop lettuce, watercress, endive and romaine in very fine pieces, using a knife or food processor. Mix chopped ingredients together in one large wide bowl, or in individual wide shallow bowls. Add chives. Arrange tomatoes, chicken, bacon, avocado and eggs in narrow strips or wedges across top of greens. Sprinkle with cheese. Chill. At serving time, toss with ½ cup French Dressing. Pass remaining dressing.

FRENCH DRESSING

¼ cup water
¼ cup red wine vinegar
¼ teaspoon granulated sugar
1½ teaspoons lemon juice
½ teaspoon salt
½ teaspoon black pepper
½ teaspoon Worcestershire sauce
¾ teaspoon dry mustard
½ clove garlic, minced
¼ cup olive oil
¾ cup vegetable oil

Combine water, vinegar, sugar, lemon juice, salt, pepper, Worcestershire sauce, mustard, garlic and oils in a container with lid. Shake well before using.

MINUTE MAN SHRIMP SALAD

1 pound shrimp, cooked and peeled
¼ cup green onion, chopped
¼ cup celery, chopped
1 hard cooked egg, diced
Garlic Powder
Dill weed
Salt
Pepper
½ to 1 cup mayonnaise

Mix all ingredients together, chill and serve alone or stuff into tomatoes.

NEW YORK DELI SALAD

1   12-ounce package spiral pasta
1¼ cups ripe olives, pitted and sliced
1   cup red or green pepper, chopped
¼   pound hard salami, cut in thin
    strips
1   small red onion, thin rings
½   cup Parmesan cheese, grated
¼   cup parsley, chopped
¾   cup Italian Dressing

Cook pasta according to directions. In large bowl, combine olives, salami, onion, cheese, peppers, parsley and dressing. Add pasta and toss well. Serve at room temperature or chilled.
Serves: 6

BRYCE CANYON MAC SALAD

1   14-ounce package shell macaroni
3   medium tomatoes, cubed
1   medium green pepper, diced
2   medium cucumbers, diced
¾   cup Cheddar cheese, finely diced
6   green onions, chopped
1   cup mayonnaise
¾   cup milk
2   tablespoons sugar

Boil macaroni in salted water until tender. Drain; rinse with cold water. When cool, toss in salad bowl with tomatoes, green pepper, cucumbers, cheese and onions. Mix mayonnaise, milk and sugar. Stir into macaroni mixture. Cover salad and refrigerate for at least 2 hours. Stir before serving.
Serves: 6 to 8

YELLOWSTONE CHICKEN SALAD

4   cups chicken, cooked and cubed
1   cup celery, chopped
1   cup seedless green grapes, halved
1   teaspoon salt
¼   teaspoon pepper
¾   cup mayonnaise
¼   cup sour cream
1   cup mixed nuts, coarsley
    chopped
Crisp lettuce

Combine chicken, celery and grapes in large bowl. Sprinkle with salt and pepper. Add mayonnaise and sour cream; mix thoroughly. Chill. Toss nuts lightly with chicken. Serve on lettuce.
Serves: 8

MUIR WOODS VEGETABLE SALAD

1   9-ounce package frozen cut green beans, cooked and drained
1   9-ounce package frozen artichoke hearts, cooked and drained
1   6-ounce can sliced mushrooms, drained
1   8-ounce jar green olives, drained and sliced
2   small onions, sliced
1   clove garlic, minced
⅓   cup white or tarragon vinegar
½   cup olive oil
1   teaspoon salt
¼   teaspoon pepper

Combine all ingredients and marinate overnight. Serve chilled. Serves 8

KENNEDY CRAB MEAT SALAD

2   7-ounce cans crabmeat
2   cups rice, cooked and cooled
8   ounces green peas
1½ cups celery, finely sliced
¼   cup pimentos, sliced
1   cup mayonnaise
1½ tablespoons lemon juice
1   teaspoon salt
¼   teaspoon pepper

Combine crabmeat, rice, celery, peas and pimentos. Combine remaining ingredients; pour over crabmeat mixture. Toss lightly. May add more seasonings at this point. Chill and serve on lettuce leaves. Serves: 6

KINGS CANYON AVOCADO SALAD

⅔   cup salad oil
¼   cup wine vinegar
1   teaspoon salt
⅛   teaspoon pepper
⅛   teaspoon Tabasco sauce
⅓   cup green chiles, chopped
¼   cup pimientos, chopped
4   ripe avocados, chopped
4   tomatoes, chopped
4   green onions, chopped
1   head lettuce

Mix oil, vinegar, salt, pepper and Tabasco sauce together in a bottle and shake well. Add chiles and pimientos. Combine avocados, tomatoes and green onions. Spoon onto bed of lettuce. Pour dressing over top and serve. Serves: 8

HOT BACON DRESSING

Assorted salad greens
6 slices bacon, fried and crumbled
6 tablespoons bacon drippings
6 tablespoons vinegar
6 tablespoons water
6 tablespoons sugar
1 egg

In skillet, combine bacon drippings, vinegar, water and sugar. Heat to boiling; cool slightly. Beat egg in a bowl and stir slowly into warm vinegar mixture. Add bacon crumbles and cook slowly for 5 minutes. Serve hot over fresh spinach or favorite greens. Add few raisins if desired.

DENALI LOW FAT DRESSING

1 package low-fat Ranch salad dressing mix
1½ cups skim milk
¼ cup fat-free mayonnaise

Combine all ingredients in small bowl; stir until smooth. Cover and chill.
Yield: 2 cups

MESA VERDE BLEU DRESSING

1 cup sour cream
1 cup mayonnaise
1 tablespoon Worcestershire sauce
1 teaspoon garlic salt
2 green onions, chopped
1 package bleu cheese

Set cheese out to soften. Mix everything by mixer except bleu cheese. Crumble bleu cheese and combine with creamy mixture.

ITALIAN DRESSING

¾ cup olive oil
½ cup red wine vinegar
1 tablespoon grated Parmesan cheese
1 garlic clove, minced
½ teaspoon salt
½ teaspoon sugar
½ teaspoon dried oregano
Dash pepper

Combine all ingredients in tight fitting jar; shake well. Refrigerate.
Yield: 1¼ cups

STATUE OF LIBERTY NATIONAL MONUMENT

The Statue of Liberty, one of the United States' most famous monuments, if not its most famous, stands visible to all on Liberty Island in New York Harbor. This statue is "the" monument which symbolizes America to most Americans and others from around the world. It was a gift to the American people from the citizens of France in 1886 in commemoration of the friendship between the two nations during the American Revolution. It was the support and action of the French that contributed to the liberation of the American Colonies from England.

The concept of such a monument was proposed by Edouard de Laboulaye, a French historian and commentator. Its designer and producer was Frederic Auguste Bartholdi. Bartholdi also chose New York harbor as the site of his impressive statue. Knowing that immigrant ancestors of many Americans entered through the harbor, he considered it the gateway to America.

Bartholdi, in creating his statue, did not have a simple task. Molding first a nine foot model, then fabricating larger models, allowed him to reach the scale and detail of the statue seen today. Standing 152 feet tall, the statue is basically a hollow figure of external copper sheets, about the thickness of a silver dollar, on an interior steel support frame. Stairs or an elevator provide visitor access to the top of the statue's pedestal. A spiral stairway allows access from the pedestal to the crown.

Continuing love for this magnificent lady was easily demonstrated when people from all around the world provided the funds for her complete restoration on her 100th birthday.

In a visit to New York, plan to see the statue. It will be an experience you will always remember.

STATUE OF LIBERTY

Scotty's Castle, *Death Valley National Park*, is the home of a famous prospector in the desert in California.

Delaware Water Gap National Recreation Area, PA provides a scenic area on both the New Jersey and Pennsylvania sides of the Delaware River.

Denali National Park, AK, contains North America's highest mountain, Mount McKinley, at 20,320 feet.

The nation's first national monument, *Devils Tower National Monument*, WY exhibits an 865 foot tower of volcanic columnar rock.

Dinosaur National Monument, CO has spectacular canyon scenery and a quarry containing fossil remains of dinosaurs and other ancient animals.

Thomas Edison, inventor of the light bulb, worked and lived at the *Edison National Historic Site*, NJ from 1887 until 1931.

Native Americans fashioned their mounds in the images of birds and animals for the Effigy culture at *Effigy Mounds National Monument*, IA.

Eisenhower National Historic Site, PA contains the only home General Dwight D. Eisenhower and his wife, Mamie, owned. The home served as a presidential retreat, then retirement home for the president and his wife.

Inscription Rock, *El Morro National Monument*, NM rises 200 feet from the valley floor, on which ancient carved inscriptions can be seen.

Everglades National Park, FL has countless creatures that breed and feed on this watery land. The park is a favorite for bird lovers. Alligators, crocodiles, and other tropical wildlife, such as manatees, may be seen.

George Washington took his oath as the first U.S. President at *Federal Hall National Memorial*, NY on April 30, 1789.

Fire Island National Seashore, NY is known for its marvelous beaches, dunes, Fire Island Light, and the estate of William Floyd, a signer of the Declaration of Independence. Located one hour from New York City makes this park accessible for visitors.

President Abraham Lincoln was shot on April 14, 1865 while attending the comedy "Our American Cousin" at Ford's Theatre, which is now *Ford's Theatre National Historic Site*, Washington, D.C. The theatre looks very much the same as that tragic night with the president's box festooned with the nation's flag.

SHENANDOAH NATIONAL PARK

The fort at *Fort Davis National Historic Site*, TX was named for Jefferson Davis, Secretary of War, later President of the Confederacy.

Francis Scott Key who wrote "The Star Spangled Banner" was inspired to do so by observing the defense of Fort McHenry, now *Fort McHenry National Monument*, MD in the War of 1812.

Fort Smith National Historic Site, AR was one of the first U.S. military posts in the Louisiana Territory. Judge Isaac C. Parker served 21 years protecting Native American rights at this quaint Arkansas post.

The first military engagement of the Civil War took place at *Fort Sumter National Monument*, SC on April 12, 1861.

Frederick Douglass National Historic Site, Washington, D.C., was the home of the nation's leading African American spokesman from 1877 to 1895.

Fredericksburg & Spotsylvania National Military Park, VA was the site of four major battles fought in the Civil War: Fredericksburg, Chancellorsville, Wilderness, and Spotsylvania.

Gateway National Recreation Area, NY has forts, wildlife sanctuaries, the oldest operating lighthouse and numerous other facilities which provide recreational and educational opportunities around New York Harbor.

George Washington Birthplace National Monument, VA, the birthplace of the first U.S. President, contains tombs of Washington's ancestors and a memorial mansion with gardens.

George Washington Carver National Monument, MO honors the famous black agriculturist, educator and humanitarian.

Gettysburg National Military Park, PA is the site of a great Civil War battle on July 1-3, 1863, that left 51,000 Union and Confederate soldiers dead. On November 19, 1863, President Abraham Lincoln delivered his memorable Gettysburg address at the dedication of the National Cemetery.

By boat or plane, *Glacier Bay National Park and Preserve*, AK offers magnificent glaciers, lush vegetation and unlimited wildlife.

Glacier National Park, MT has one million acres in the heart of the Rocky Mountains. Its mountains, glaciers and lakes are total natural grandeur. The Going-to-the-Sun Road is one of the outstanding mountain passes in the country. It is wise to avoid the grizzly bears.

Lake Powell, at *Glen Canyon National Recreation Area* , AZ is an exceptional spot to vacation by houseboat in the rugged canyon country.

Main Dishes

CHICKEN BREAST SEQUOIA

8   to 10 chicken breasts
1   package fine bread crumbs
1   package taco seasoning
1   quart half and half
8   ounces shredded Monterey Jack
    cheese
8   ounces shredded Cheddar cheese
1   4-ounce can green chilies

Mix bread crumbs and taco seasoning. Roll each piece of chicken in mixture and place in roaster. Combine half and half with next 3 ingredients and pour over chicken. Bake at 350 degrees for 1 hour.

YOSEMITE CHICKEN PARMESAN

2   boneless chicken breasts
2   cloves of garlic, mashed
½   stick butter
½   cup sour cream
Paprika
½   cup Parmesan cheese, grated
½   teaspoon salt
⅛   teaspoon pepper

Pound chicken breasts slightly to flatten. Heat garlic in butter to melt; cool slightly. Mix half of garlic butter with sour cream. Spread sour cream mixture over each chicken breast. Roll in Parmesan mixed with salt and pepper. Place chicken in foil lined baking dish. Sprinkle with paprika. Bake uncovered in 375 degree oven 30 minutes. Baste often with remaining garlic butter. During last 5 minutes, broil swiftly to brown cheese. Garnish with lemon slices. Also can be topped with sliced mozzarella, then spaghetti sauce.

GLACIER OVEN FRIED CHICKEN

1½ cups potato chips, finely crushed
1   teaspoon chili powder
1   chicken, cut up
¼   cup margarine, melted

Brush chicken pieces with margarine; roll in potato chip mixture. Line a cookie sheet with foil; arrange chicken pieces so pieces don't touch. Pepper chicken. Bake at 375 degrees for 55 minutes. Do not turn chicken.

PINNACLES SPINACH-CHICKEN FETTUCINI

2   tablespoons butter
1   chicken breast, cut into strips
2   tablespoons flour
Salt, pepper and tarragon
1   tablespoon green onion, diced
¼   cup mushrooms, sliced
2   teaspoons lemon juice
½   cup cream
2   cups spinach fettucini, cooked
¼   cup Parmesan cheese
2   tablespoons tomatoes, diced

Heat butter in skillet. Dredge chicken in seasoned flour. Saute' chicken for 30 seconds. Add green onions, mushrooms and lemon juice. Continue to saute' until chicken is lightly browned. Add cream, pasta, Parmesan cheese and tomatoes. Stir gently to combine thoroughly. Simmer until cream thickens. Serves: 2

POLLO BOSCAIOLA

8   6-ounce boneless, chicken breasts, skinned
Salt
Pepper
1   16-ounce can artichoke hearts, drained and quartered
¾   pounds fresh mushrooms, quartered
5   garlic cloves, finely minced
2   cups white wine
1   cup whipping cream
1   16-ounce can tomato sauce
1   to 1½ pounds spinach linguini noodles

Mix flour, salt and pepper. Dredge chicken and saute' in a small amount of margarine on one side until brown. Turn chicken and add vegetables. When vegetables are half cooked, add garlic; cook until golden brown. Add wine, and cook 5 minutes, remove chicken and vegetables; cool wine slightly, then stir in cream and tomato sauce and cook until mixture thickens. Add chicken and vegetables. Serve over linguini and garnish with parsley and basil.

CHICKEN ENCHILADA

1   cup onion, chopped
1   tablespoon oil
3   cups chicken, cooked and diced
2   4-ounce cans green chiles, chopped
½   pound Cheddar cheese, shredded
½   pound Monterey Jack cheese, shredded
12   corn tortillas
Oil
1   can cream of chicken soup
2   8-ounce cartons sour cream

Saute' onion in oil. Add chicken, chiles, and ⅔ of each cheese. Fry tortillas quickly in hot oil to soften and drain on paper towels. Divide chicken mixture evenly among tortillas. Roll up and place in a greased 9x13-inch baking dish. Combine soup and sour cream. Pour over enchilada and top with remaining cheese. Bake 20-30 minutes in a 350 degree oven. Serves: 6

OLD FAITHFUL LIGHT CHICKEN

2   onion slices (divided into rings)
2   chicken breast halves, boneless
    and skinless
Basil leaves, paprika, salt and pepper
1   medium carrot, cut in strips
½   cup zucchini, sliced
4   fresh mushrooms, sliced
1   tablespoon margarine
1   tablespoon water

Preheat oven to 450 degrees. Place onion rings on 12x18-inch sheet of aluminum foil. Place chicken on onion; sprinkle with basil, paprika, salt and pepper. Top with vegetables, margarine and water. Sprinkle with additional basil, salt and pepper to taste. Fold aluminum foil over and seal edges. Place foil packet on cookie sheet. Cook 18 minutes. Serves: 1

OLYMPIC CHICKEN-BEAN CASSEROLE

1   package wild rice
3   cups chicken, cooked and diced
½   cup mayonnaise
¼   cup onion, minced
1   can celery soup
½   cup water
1   can french green beans, drained
1   can water chestnuts, drained
1   stick margarine
2   cups dry herb stuffing

Mix first 8 ingredients together. Put in 9x13-inch casserole dish. Mix stuffing and melted margarine. Place on mixture; cover with foil. Bake at 375 degrees for 30 minutes. Remove foil, bake 15 minutes longer at 350 degrees.

PRESIDENT'S CHICKEN SPAGHETTI

1   hen (5 pounds or more)
4   onions, chopped
1   green pepper, chopped
½   bunch celery, chopped
1   can mushroom soup
2   cans tomato soup
1   teaspoon salt
1   tablespoon Tabasco sauce
1   cup grated cheese
2   10-ounce packages spaghetti
2   teaspoons pepper
1   stick oleo

Cook chicken and dice. Cook spaghetti. In oleo, cook onions, pepper and celery until tender. In a large bowl, add remaining ingredients. Combine all; put in large baking dish. Bake at 350 degrees for 20 minutes until bubbly. Can be frozen, thawed and heated. Serves: 12

CASHEW CHICKEN

3 whole chicken breasts, boned and
   skinned
2 6-ounce packages frozen pea pods,
   or fresh
½ pound fresh mushrooms, sliced
4 green onions, cut in 1" lengths
1 15-ounce can bamboo shoots,
   drained
1 cup chicken broth
¼ cup soy sauce
2 tablespoons cornstarch
½ teaspoon sugar
½ teaspoon salt
¼ cup sesame or peanut oil
1 cup cashews

Slice chicken in 1-inch squares. Mix chicken broth, soy sauce, cornstarch, sugar and salt together. Heat 1 table-spoon oil to high. Add nuts and cook a minute and remove from pan and set aside. Add remaining oil to pan and add chicken and cook quickly. Add peas and mushrooms; pour in broth mixture. Cover and simmer 2 minutes. Add bamboo shoots. Stir constantly until mixture thickens. Simmer 1 minute uncovered. Mix in green onions. Sprinkle with nuts and serve. Serves 4-6

OCMULGEE CHAMPAGNE CHICKEN

2 tablespoons flour
½ teaspoon salt
¼ teaspoon pepper
4 chicken breast halves, skinned and
   boned
2 tablespoons butter or margarine
1 tablespoon olive oil
¾ cup champagne or white wine
¾ cup fresh mushrooms, sliced
½ cup whipping cream

Combine flour, salt and pepper; rub all over chicken. Heat butter and oil in large skillet. Add chicken and brown about 5 minutes on each side. Add champagne and cook over medium heat 15 minutes or until done. Remove chicken and set aside. Add mushrooms and whipping cream to skillet. Cook over low heat, stirring constantly until thick. Add chicken long enough to heat through. Serves: 4

ABE LINCOLN CHICKEN

6 chicken breasts, skinless and
   deboned
1 can cream of celery soup
1 can cream of chicken soup
1 8-ounce carton sour cream
1 stick of margarine
1½ stacks of crushed Ritz crackers
Poppy seeds

Cut cooked chicken into pieces and combine with soup mixture. Melt margarine. Mix margarine and crushed crackers and put on top of chicken mixture. Sprinkle poppy seeds on top of chicken mixture. Bake at 350 degrees for 30 minutes. Serve with noodles.

HALF DOME CRAB CHICKEN

6   chicken breasts, skinned and
     boned
½   cup onion, chopped
½   cup celery, chopped
3   tablespoons butter
3   tablespoons dry white wine
1   7½-ounce can crabmeat, drained
     and flaked
½   cup herb-seasoned stuffing mix
2   tablespoons flour
½   teaspoon paprika
1   envelope hollandaise sauce mix
¾   cup milk
2   tablespoons dry white wine
½   cup (2-ounces) shredded process
     Swiss cheese

Pound chicken to flatten. Sprinkle with a little salt and pepper. Cook onion and celery in the 3 tablespoons butter until tender. Remove from heat; add the 3 tablespoons wine, the crab, and stuffing mix; toss. Divide mixture among breasts. Roll up and secure. Combine flour and paprika; coat chicken. Place in 11x7x1-inch baking dish; drizzle with 2 tablespoons melted butter. Bake, uncovered, in 375 degree oven for 1 hour. Transfer to platter. Blend sauce mix and milk; cook and stir until thick. Add remaining wine and cheese; stir until cheese melts. Pour some on chicken; pass remaining. Serves: 6

VANDERBILT CHICKEN MARSALA

4   chicken breasts, boneless and
     skinless
1   tablespoon margarine
¼   cup flour
⅛   teaspoon salt
Pepper
1   cup mushrooms, sliced
½   teaspoon garlic, minced
½   cup chicken broth
½   cup Marsala wine

Flatten chicken breast; cut in half. Melt margarine in skillet. Combine flour, salt and pepper. Dip chicken in flour mixture and coat evenly. Saute' chicken for 1-2 minutes until golden on each side. Add mushrooms, garlic, chicken broth and Marsala wine. Continue to cook for 2 minutes until mushrooms are tender. Place mixture on platter and pour juices over chicken. Serve immediately.

CUYAHOGA CHICKEN NOODLE CASSEROLE

1   stewing chicken
1   large onion
1   pound noodles
1   pound Velveeta cheese
2   cans undiluted mushroom soup
1   can button mushrooms
Buttered bread crumbs

Stew chicken with large onion. Remove from pan, cool and debone chicken. Cook noodles in broth until broth is absorbed. Mix noodles and chicken with cheese and soup. Add mushrooms; top with bread crumbs. Bake at 350 degrees for 45-60 minutes. Serves: 12

CAPE HATTERAS COFFEE ROAST

1 tablespoon cooking oil
1 eye of round beef roast (about 2½ pounds)
1 medium onion, chopped
1 cup brewed coffee
1 cup water, divided
1 beef bouillon cube
2 teaspoons dried basil
1 teaspoon dried rosemary
1 garlic clove, minced
1 teaspoon salt
½ teaspoon pepper
¼ cup all-purpose flour

Heat oil in Dutch oven; brown roast on all sides. Add onion and cook until transparent. Add coffee, ¾ cup water, bouillon, basil, rosemary, garlic, salt and pepper. Cover and simmer for 2½ hours or until meat is tender. Combine flour and remaining water until smooth; stir into pan juices. Cook and stir until thickened and bubbly. Remove roast and slice. Pass the gravy. Serves: 8

MOUNT RUSHMORE ROAST

1 rump roast
1 can Coca Cola
1 package dry onion soup mix

Pour mixture over roast and bake for 4 hours at 275 degrees. The liquid is delicious gravy.

BEEF BRISKET/BAR B Q SAUCE

4 pounds brisket
1 onion, sliced
1 lemon, sliced
BAR B Q SAUCE
2 cups catsup
2 tablespoons Worcestershire sauce
¼ teaspoon hot sauce
2 teaspoons dry mustard
1 teaspoon salt
2 tablespoons liquid smoke
¼ cup brown sugar

Put onions and lemons on top of meat and place in baking dish. Bake in 250 degree oven for 6 hours. Trim fat when cool. Slice brisket and cover with sauce. Bake 30 minutes in oven.

SQUAW CREEK TACO PEPPERS

1   pound ground beef
1   1¼-ounce package taco seasoning
   mix
1   8-ounce can kidney beans, rinsed
   and drained
1   cup salsa
4   medium green peppers
1   medium tomato, chopped
½   cup shredded Cheddar cheese
½   cup sour cream

In a large skillet, brown ground beef; drain. Stir in taco seasoning, kidney beans and salsa. Bring to a boil; reduce heat and simmer for 5 minutes. Cut peppers in half lengthwise; remove and discard seeds and stems. Immerse peppers in boiling water for 3 minutes; drain. Spoon about ½ cup meat mixture into each pepper half. Place in an ungreased 13x9x2-inch baking dish. Cover and bake at 350 degrees for 15-20 minutes or until peppers are crisp-tender and filling is heated through. Top each with tomato, cheese and a dollop of sour cream. Serves: 4

CABRILLO TACO CASSEROLE

1   8-ounce package Jiffy Corn
   Muffin Mix
1   pound ground chuck
1   small onion, chopped
1   package taco seasoning mix
1   16-ounce can tomatoes, drained
1   4-ounce package shredded sharp
   Cheddar cheese

Prepare corn muffin mix according to package directions. Spoon into greased (bottom only) 8x8x2-inch glass dish. Set aside while preparing remainder of casserole. Saute' ground chuck and onion together; pour off fat. Add taco mix and drained tomatoes. Cook 5 minutes, then spoon into muffin batter. Top with shredded cheese. Bake at 375 degrees for about 25 minutes.

NAVAJO TACOS

1   pound hamburger
1   small can chili with beans
1   large onion, chopped
1   can whole chilis
Shredded Lettuce
Diced tomatoes (fresh)
Grated Cheddar cheese
FRY BREAD (for Tacos)
4   cups flour
1   tablespoon baking powder
1   teaspoon salt
2   tablespoons shortening
2   tablespoons powdered milk
1½ cups warm water

Fry hamburger, add chili and beans, simmer until well blended.
FRY BREAD: Combine flour, baking powder, salt and powdered milk, add shortening and blend. Add water and mix with hands until soft. Make flat circle of dough and deep fry until brown on both sides.
TO SERVE: Place fried fry bread on plate, cover top with chili and meat mixture, then add in order given: shredded lettuce, chopped onion, chopped tomatoes, shredded cheese and top with one whole green chili.

SARATOGA SPAGHETTI BAKE

12	ounce package spaghetti
1	pound ground beef
1	small onion
1	can cream of mushroom soup
1	can cream style corn
1	pint tomato juice
2	teaspoons cumin
1	tablespoon chili powder

American cheese

Cook spaghetti; drain. Saute' beef and onion; drain. In blender, mix soup, corn, juice and seasonings. Combine together and place in 9x13-inch baking dish. Place cheese on top and bake at 350 degrees until cheese melts and dish is heated through.

PEPPER LONDON BROIL

1	beef flank steak (about ¾ pound)
1	garlic clove, minced
½	teaspoon seasoned salt
⅛	teaspoon crushed red pepper
¼	cup Worcestershire sauce

With meat fork, poke holes in both sides of meat. Make a paste with garlic, seasoned salt and red pepper; rub over both sides of meat. Place the steak in a gallon-size plastic bag. Add Worcestershire sauce and close bag. Refrigerate for at least 4 hours, turning once. Remove meat; discard marinade. Broil or grill over hot coals until meat reaches desired doneness, 4-5 minutes per side. To serve, slice thinly across grain.
Serves: 2

INDEPENDENCE PORK CHOPS

6	pork chops
½	cup chicken broth
½	cup honey
¼	cup soy sauce
2	tablespoons catsup
¼	teaspoon ginger
1	garlic clove, minced

Brown pork chops in skillet. Mix other ingredients. Pour over pork chops. Cover and cook over low heat for 30-45 minutes. Spoon mixture over chops several times while cooking. Serve with rice. Electric skillet works best.

PORK PICCATA

1	pork tenderloin
½	cup flour
½	teaspoon salt
¼	teaspoon pepper
3	tablespoons olive oil
½	cup dry white wine
⅓	cup lemon juice
3	tablespoons margarine
¼	cup parsley
1½	tablespoons capers

Cut tenderloin into 2-ounce medallions. Between sheets of wax paper, flatten each medallion to ¼-inch thick. Combine flour, salt and pepper. Dredge pork in mixture. Cook half of pork in 1½ tablespoons oil in large skillet over medium heat, about 2 minutes on each side, remove; repeat with other half, remove. Add wine and lemon juice to skillet; heat thoroughly. Add margarine, parsley and capers; replace meat, heat and serve. TO SERVE: Arrange pork over cooked pasta, drizzle with wine mixture and garnish with parsley and lemon slices.

GREAT SMOKIES HAM LOAF

½	pound ground ham
½	pound pork sausage
½	pound ground beef
1	cup evaporated milk
¼	cup catsup
2	tablespoons onion, chopped
¾	teaspoons dry mustard
¾	cup soft bread crumbs
1	teaspoon salt
¼	teaspoon pepper
½	cup brown sugar
2	tablespoons vinegar
2	tablespoons water

Combine meats, milk, catsup, onion, mustard, bread crumbs, salt and pepper. Mix thoroughly. Shape into loaf. Bake in greased pan, in oven pre-heated to 350 degrees for 30 minutes. Drain off grease. Mix together brown sugar, vinegar and water. Pour over loaf and return meat to oven. Continue to bake about one hour longer. Baste frequently with glaze in bottom of pan. Let loaf set about 10 minutes before slicing.
Serves: 6

FRUITY HAM GLAZE

¼	cup cranberry-orange sauce
¼	cup apricot or peach preserves

About 30 minutes before ham is done, remove from oven. Score surface; spoon glaze over entire ham. Return to oven, basting occasionally during the last 30 minutes of baking. Yield: ½ cup.

PINEAPPLE HAM GLAZE

½ cup crushed pineapple
¼ cup Dijon mustard
Dash ground cloves

Combine all ingredients in small bowl. About 30 minutes before ham is done, remove from the oven. Score surface; spoon glaze over entire ham. Return to oven, basting occasionally during the last 30 minutes of baking. Yield: ½ cup.

TRUMAN PORK 'N' RICE

2 pounds lean pork steaks
1 garlic clove, chopped
10 green onions, chopped
1 teaspoon black pepper
½ teaspoon red pepper
¼ cup soy sauce
¼ cup water
1 6-ounce jar sliced mushrooms
4 cups rice, cooked
Salt to taste

Cut pork into ½-inch cubes. Chop garlic and green onions. Saute' pork, garlic and onions until pork is browned. Add salt, pepper, soy sauce and water. Simmer on low heat for 20 minutes. Cook rice. Serve pork over rice.

PAINTED DESERT TENDERLOIN

1 pork tenderloin strip roast
⅛ cup Worcestershire sauce
2 garlic cloves, chopped
1 tablespoon brown sugar
1 tablespoon butter, melted

Place Worcestershire sauce, garlic and pork in zip lock plastic bag. Marinade for 2 hours. Grill until done to your liking. Add brown sugar and butter to remaining marinade and baste pork last few minutes. Remove and serve.

BISCAYNE PORK CHOP-POTATOES

3 tablespoons butter
3 tablespoons flour
1½ teaspoons salt
¼ teaspoons pepper
1 can chicken broth
6 pork chops
2 tablespoons oil
6 cups potatoes, peeled and sliced
1 onion, sliced
Salt, pepper, paprika, parsley to taste

Melt butter; add flour, salt and pepper. Add broth; cook and stir until mixture boils. Cook for 1 minute, remove from heat. Brown pork chops in oiled skillet; season to taste. Layer potatoes and onion in 9x13-inch casserole. Pour broth mixture over. Place chops on top. Cover and bake 1 hour; uncover, bake 30 minutes more. Sprinkle with parsley and paprika for color. Serves: 6

GULF ISLANDS VEAL PICCATA

8   veal strips, 3-inches long, 1-inch
    wide
⅛   pound butter
Juice of one lemon
Few capers
1   egg, slightly beaten
Salt and pepper
4   eggplant slices
Bread crumbs

Saute' veal in butter. Add lemon juice
and capers. Meanwhile mix beaten egg,
salt and pepper. Dip eggplant in egg
mixture. Cover with bread crumbs and
fry in butter. Serve veal on top of
eggplant; slice and garnish with lemon.
Serves: 4

FIRE ISLAND SCALLOPPINE MARSALA

½   cup flour
1   teaspoon salt
Pepper
1   teaspoon lemon rind
1   pound veal, thinly sliced, cut in
    2½-inch pieces
¼   pound butter
4   tablespoons Marsala wine
4   teaspoons chicken broth

Combine flour, salt, pepper and lemon
rind. Meanwhile pound veal flat and cut
in 2½-inch pieces. Coat veal with flour
mixture. Brown veal in buttered skillet
about 3 minutes on each side. Heat wine
and broth in saucepan over low heat.
When veal is browned, spoon the
Marsala-chicken broth over veal.
Serves: 4

NORTH CASCADES LAMB

1   5-pound leg of lamb
1   8-ounce jar Dijon mustard
⅓   cup dry white wine
¼   cup oil
2   cloves garlic, minced
1   teaspoon dried rosemary, crushed
1   teaspoon dried basil, crushed
½   teaspoon dried oregano, crushed
½   teaspoon dried thyme, crushed
¼   teaspoon pepper

For marinade: In a mixing bowl,
combine mustard, wine, oil, garlic,
rosemary, basil, oregano, thyme, and
pepper.
Place lamb in shallow dish, and spread
with marinade. Cover; marinate 1 hour
at room temperature. Drain meat but
reserve the marinade. Skewer the lamb
for grilling. Place meat on grill above
drip pan, not over coals. Grill for 1 to
1½ hours until slightly pink in center.
During last 15 minutes of grilling, brush
with marinade.

TURKEY STIR FRY CANYONLANDS

1½ pound raw boneless turkey, cut
    into strips
1   tablespoon cooking oil
1   small onion, chopped
1   carrot, julienned
½ medium green pepper, sliced
2   cups fresh mushrooms, sliced
1   cup chicken broth
3   tablespoons cornstarch
3   tablespoons soy sauce
½ teaspoon ground ginger
2   cups pea pods, trimmed
Cooked rice, optional
⅓ cup cashews, optional

In a large skillet or wok, stir-fry turkey in oil over medium-high heat until no longer pink, about 5-6 minutes. Remove turkey and keep warm. Stir-fry the onion, carrot, green pepper and mushrooms until crisp-tender, about 5 minutes. In a small bowl, combine chicken broth, cornstrach, soy sauce and ginger. Add to skillet; cook and stir until thickened and bubbly. Return turkey to skillet with pea pods; cook and stir until heated through. If desired, serve over rice and top with cashews. Serves: 6

OZARK EASY SMOKED TURKEY

1   medium turkey, thawed
2   quarts water
1   bottle Natural Hickory Liquid
    Smoke

Mix water and liquid smoke for marinade. Place bird and marinade in large plastic bag. Leave for 24 hours in refrigerator. Remove turkey, roast your favorite way.

SCHOODIC HOT TURKEY SALAD

2   cups turkey, cooked and cubed
2   cups celery, chopped
½ cup almonds, blanched and
    chopped
⅓ cup green pepper, chopped
2   tablespoons pimiento, chopped
2   tablespoons onion, chopped
1   teaspoon salt
2   tablespoons lemon juice
½ cup mayonnaise
Swiss cheese, sliced
½ stick butter, melted
1   cup cracker crumbs

Combine turkey, celery, almonds, green pepper, pimiento, onion, salt, lemon juice and mayonnaise. Spoon into buttered 1½ quart casserole. Top with slice of cheese. Combine butter and cracker crumbs. Sprinkle on top of casserole. Bake at 350 degrees for 30 minutes.

ROCKY MOUNTAIN LAKE TROUT

Dress freshly caught lake trout by splitting down stomach, cleaning, cutting open along backbone and lay on buttered broiler pan skin side down.

Dot with butter and broil slowly at 400 degrees so tail does not curl. Broiling time approximately 15 minutes.

HOT SPRINGS FRIED CATFISH

3   pounds catfish fillets
1   cup yellow corn meal
1   teaspoon salt
1½ teaspoons paprika
½   teaspoon pepper
½   teaspoon onion powder
¼   teaspoon dry mustard

Mix cornmeal and seasonings. Roll fish in meal mix. Place fish in hot oil in skillet. Fry on medium heat for 5 minutes or until brown. Turn carefully. Fry 5 minutes longer. Remove from heat and drain well on paper towels. Serve with Tartar Sauce.

TARTAR SAUCE

½   cup salad dressing
1   teaspoon sugar
1   teaspoon mustard
2   tablespoons pickle relish
1   tablespoon lemon juice
¼   teaspoon onion
¼   teaspoon Worcestershire sauce

Combine all ingredients; mix to blend. Serve chilled with favorite fish dish.

GRANT'S FISH BATTER

1   cup pancake mix
1   cup club soda

Combine mix and soda. Wet fish with water, flour and let rest five minutes. Dip in batter and fry in hot oil.

GLACIER BAY HALIBUT

2 pounds haddock fillets
1 cup seasoned dry bread crumbs
¼ cup butter or margarine, melted
2 tablespoons dried parsley flakes
2 teaspoons grated lemon
½ teaspoon garlic powder

Cut fish into serving-size pieces. Place in a greased 11x7x2-inch baking dish. Combine remaining ingredients; sprinkle over fish. Bake at 350 degrees for 25 minutes or until fish flakes easily with a fork. Serves: 6

BAKED STUFFED FLOUNDER

6 baby flounder, boned or 6 flounder fillets
Seafood dressing
Salt and pepper to taste
3 tablespoons lemon juice
1 cup fine bread crumbs
⅓ pound butter, melted

Preheat oven to 375 degrees. Grease shallow baking pan. Stuff each fish with 4 to 6 tablespoons of seafood dressing, or spread same amount over each fillet. Roll and fasten with toothpicks. Place in pan, season with salt, pepper and lemon juice. Sprinkle bread crumbs over fish. Melt butter and pour over fish. Bake at 375 degrees for 25-30 minutes or until fish flakes when tested with a fork.

SEAFOOD DRESSING

6 tablespoons butter
¼ cup celery, finely chopped
½ cup onion, finely chopped
¼ cup green pepper, finely chopped
½ pound shrimp, cooked and diced
1 teaspoon parsley, chopped
1 teaspoon pimiento, finely chopped
½ teaspoon paprika
1 teaspoon Worcestershire sauce
½ teaspoon seafood seasoning
Salt to taste
⅛ teaspoon cayenne pepper
¼ cup dry sherry
1½ cups bread crumbs

Melt butter; add the vegetables and saute' until tender. Add all of the remaining ingredients except bread crumbs to the vegetables and cook over low heat for 10 minutes. Add this mixture to the bread crumbs and mix thoroughly.

HAWAII VOLCANOES SHRIMP

Batter:
½ cup flour
¼ cup cornstarch
½ teaspoon salt
½ cup water
1 egg white
Dipping Sauce:
½ cup honey
3 tablespoons horseradish
1 pound large shrimp, peeled
2½ cups flaked coconut
1 cup oil, for frying

Mix batter ingredients in small bowl. Dip shrimp, then roll in coconut to coat. Place on waxed paper. Heat oil in skillet. Fry shrimp about 8 at one time, until crisp, golden, about one minute on each side. Drain on paper towels. Serve hot with dipping sauce. Makes eight appetizer servings.

POINT REYES SCAMPI

12 jumbo shrimp, shelled, deveined and butterflied
1 stick unsalted butter
1 teaspoon shallots, minced
1 garlic clove, minced
1 lemon, juiced
1 teaspoon A-1 sauce
½ teaspoon Worcestershire sauce
½ teaspoon tarragon
Dash Tabasco sauce and black pepper

Place shrimp tails up in buttered shallow pan. Bake at 400 degrees for 2 minutes. Remove from oven and set aside. Melt butter, add seasonings. Remove from heat and cool, stirring often to blend flavors. Spread mixture over shrimp. Place shrimp mixture under broiler for 2 or 3 minutes. Serves: 2

BLACK CANYON TROUT

½ cup butter, softened
⅛ cup parsley, chopped
⅛ cup watercress, chopped
1 tablespoon dill seed
1½ teaspoon lemon juice
⅛ teaspoon black pepper

Combine all ingredients. Take a 12-inch piece of foil, spread butter mixture lengthwise in a one-inch strip. Freeze for one hour. Broil trout meat side up for 6 minutes. Place cold butter on trout to serve.

53

SAINT CROIX SHRIMP CURRY

2   tablespoons butter
½   cup onion, chopped finely
½   cup apple, peeled and finely
    chopped
2   teaspoons curry powder
1   can frozen cream of shrimp soup
1   cup sour cream
1   cup cooked shrimp

Melt butter in saucepan. Add onion, apple and curry powder. Simmer until tender. Stir in soup and bring to a boil, then add sour cream and shrimp. Heat to boiling but don't boil. Serve over rice.

ASSATEAGUE SCALLOPS

1   pint scallops
½   cup butter
1   cup cracker crumbs
½   cup soft bread crumbs
⅔   cup cream
Salt and pepper to taste

Wash and look over scallops. Melt butter, add cracker and bread crumbs. Put layer of crumbs in buttered baking dish, cover with scallops, half the cream. Season to taste, repeat; cover with buttered crumbs. Bake 25 minutes at 350 degrees.

ROOSEVELT BAKED LOBSTER

Prepare lobster for broiling. Dot meat with butter; sprinkle with salt, pepper and ¼ cup buttered bread crumbs. Place in baking dish. Cover and bake in a 425 degree oven for 35 minutes, basting once with melted butter. Directions for one lobster only.

ARKANSAS OVEN-FRIED CATFISH

4   catfish fillets, 6-ounces each
¼   cup yellow cornmeal
¼   cup dry bread crumbs
½   teaspoon paprika
¼   teaspoon pepper
⅛   teaspoon garlic powder
½   cup skim milk
2   tablespoons margarine, melted

Heat oven to 450 degrees. Mix cornmeal, bread crumbs, paprika, pepper and garlic powder. Dip fish in milk, coat with cornmeal mixture. Place fish in 9x12-inch pan coated with vegetable cooking spray. Pour margarine over fish. Bake uncovered until fish flakes with fork, about 18 minutes. Serves: 4

JEAN LAFITTE SHRIMP & VEGETABLES

½   cup frozen green beans
¾   cup frozen cut corn
¼   pound large raw shrimp (peeled)
¾   cup fresh snow peas
1   tablespoon margarine
1   tablespoon water
1   teaspoon lemon juice
Dash parsley flakes, salt and pepper

Preheat oven to 450 degrees. Place green beans, corn and shrimp in a single layer on 12x18-inch sheet of aluminum foil. Top with snow peas, margarine, water and lemon juice. Sprinkle on parsley, salt and pepper. Fold aluminum foil over and seal edges. Place foil packet on cookie sheet. Bake 16 minutes. Serves: 1

CHESAPEAKE CRAB

4   cans (about 8-ounces each) crabmeat
1   egg
⅔   cup green pepper, finely diced
¼   cup pimiento, finely diced
2   teaspoons dry mustard
2   teaspoons salt
¼   teaspoon white pepper
¾   cup mayonnaise or salad dressing
Paprika

Drain crabmeat; remove bony tissue, if any. Cut meat into chunks. Beat egg in a medium-sized bowl; stir in green pepper, pimiento, mustard, salt, pepper and all but 2 tablespoons of the mayonnaise or salad dressing until well blended. Fold in crabmeat. Spoon into 6 ten-ounce custard cups or individual baking dishes. Spread top of each with 1 teaspoon of the remaining mayonnaise or salad dressing; sprinkle with paprika. Bake in 350 degree oven for 15 minutes or just until hot.

CANAVERAL HOT HAM SANDWICH

¼ cup butter
2 teaspoons horseradish
2 teaspoons poppy seed
2 teaspoons onion, minced
Ham, sliced
Swiss cheese, sliced
Rolls

Mix butter, horseradish, poppy seed and onion. Spread on roll or bun; top with ham and Swiss cheese. Wrap in foil. Bake for 15 minutes at 325 degrees.

GENERAL SHERMAN BBQ SANDWICHES

1½ pound ground chuck
¾ cup celery, chopped
¾ cup onion, chopped
½ cup green pepper, chopped
1 8-ounce can tomato sauce
¼ cup catsup
2 tablespoons brown sugar
2 tablespoons BBQ sauce
2 tablespoons vinegar
1 tablespoon Worcestershire sauce
1½ teaspoons salt
¼ teaspoon pepper
1 tablespoon mustard

Brown ground chuck and drain. Set aside. Saute' celery, onion and green pepper. Mix all ingredients together and serve on buns. Serves 8 to 10

TEXAS BURGERS

3½ pounds ground beef
½ cup red cooking wine
Pepper
¼ pound butter
12 hamburger rolls
12 Bermuda onion slices
6 tablespoons chili sauce

Mix ground beef, wine and pepper. Mold into 12 patties and broil or grill until cooked to your preference. Butter rolls and toast. Top each patty with onion slice and chili sauce. Serves: 12

NEZ PERCE REUBEN SANDWICHES

8 slices dark rye or pumpernickel
  bread
3 tablespoons margarine or butter,
  softened
¼ cup Thousand Island or Russian
  salad dressing
½ pound thinly sliced cooked corned
  beef, beef, pork or ham
4 slices Swiss cheese
1 cup sauerkraut, well drained

Spread *one* side of *each* slice of bread with margarine and the other side with salad dressing. With the margarine side down, top *four* slices of bread with meat, cheese, and sauerkraut. Top with remaining bread slices, dressing side down. In a large skillet cook 2 sandwiches over medium-low heat for 4 to 6 minutes or until bread toasts and cheese melts, turning once. Repeat with remaining sandwiches. Serves: 4

BAT FLIGHT BREAKFAST

6 slices bacon, cut in pieces
3 large baking potatoes, peeled,
  cubed and cooked
½ green pepper, chopped
2 tablespoons onion, chopped
½ cup Cheddar cheese, shredded
6 eggs, beaten
Salt and pepper to taste

Cook bacon in large skillet until crisp; drain reserving 3 tablespoons drippings in skillet. Set bacon aside. Saute' potatoes, pepper and onion in drippings until potatoes are browned. Sprinkle cheese over potatoes; stir until cheese melts. Pour beaten eggs over potatoes; cook over low heat until eggs are set. Add salt and pepper to taste. Top with bacon. Serve immediately. Serves: 6

MONTEZUMA OMELET

½ cup scallions, chopped
5 tablespoons butter
½ cup green pepper, chopped
1 cup corn, drained
¾ cup ham, diced
8 eggs
½ cup milk
½ teaspoon salt
¼ teaspoon ground black pepper
2 large beefsteak tomatoes
French bread

Brown scallions and green pepper in butter; add corn and ham. Keep turning, browning slightly. Remove to warm place. Beat together eggs, milk, salt and pepper. Heat large skillet; pour in egg mixture. When eggs set, spread ham mixture on top. Loosen edge of eggs with spatula and carefully fold omelet in half. Slide onto platter. Serve with tomato slices and French bread.

GREEN CHILE QUICHE

Uncooked pastry shell
½ pound ground beef
¼ cup onion, chopped
1   4-ounce can chopped green chiles,
    drained
2   cups shredded Monterey Jack
    cheese
3   eggs, beaten
1   cup milk
¼ teaspoon salt
Dash garlic powder

Prick bottom of pastry shell and bake for 10 minutes at 375 degrees. Cool. Cook beef and onion until clear; drain each. Sprinkle into pastry; top with green chiles and cheese. Combine last 4 ingredients and pour into pie. Bake at 375 degrees for 35 minutes or until set.

JEWEL CAVE SPINACH QUICHE

1   9-inch pie crust, partially baked
2   cups heavy cream
5   eggs
½ cup Parmesan cheese, grated
¼ teaspoon thyme
½ teaspoon Tabasco sauce
¼ teaspoon nutmeg
⅛ teaspoon cayenne pepper
1   teaspoon salt
Filling:
3   cups spinach, chopped and cooked
6   ounces Gruyere cheese, grated
2   tablespoons fresh basil
1   tablespoon fresh oregano

Combine custard ingredients. Combine filling ingredients and place these on bottom of pie shell. Gently pour custard mixture over filling. Bake at 300 degrees for 45 minutes.
Hint: For a crisp, golden bottom quiche crust, pre-bake crust a bit by lining unbaked crust with 2 layers of foil. Bake at 450 degrees for 5 minutes. Remove foil and bake 5 minutes longer. Pour filling and bake according to directions.

BATHHOUSE ROW VEGETABLE STEW

1 onion, sliced
3 garlic cloves, minced
1 tablespoon olive oil
1 pound yellow squash, cubed
1 pound zucchini squash, cubed
2 medium tomatoes, peeled and
   chopped
¾ pound fresh green beans, sliced
1¼ cups frozen corn
1 teaspoon salt
¼ teaspoon pepper

In large skillet, saute' onion and garlic in oil until tender. Add squash, tomatoes and beans. Reduce heat, cover and cook slowly 15 minutes longer. Add corn, salt and pepper. Cook for 4 minutes.

YAVAPAI POTATO SOUP

1 pound ground beef
4 cups potatoes, peeled and cubed
1 small onion, chopped
3 8-ounce cans tomato sauce
4 cups water
2 teaspoons salt
1½ teaspoons pepper
½ to 1 teaspoon hot pepper sauce

In a Dutch oven or large kettle, brown ground beef. Drain. Add potatoes, onion and tomato sauce. Stir in water, salt, pepper and hot pepper sauce, bring to a boil. Reduce heat and simmer for 1 hour or until the potatoes are tender and the soup has thickened. Serves 6-8

YORKTOWN BRUNSWICK STEW

1 stewing hen (6 pounds or 2 fryers)
2 large onions, sliced
2 cups okra, cut
4 cups fresh or 2 cans (1 pound
   each) tomatoes
2 cups lima beans
4 medium potatoes, diced
2 cups fresh corn or 1 can corn
3 teaspoons salt
1 teaspoon pepper
1 tablespoon sugar
1 tablespoon dried red pepper

Cut chicken in pieces and simmer in 3 quarts water for thin stew or 2 quarts for a thick stew, until meat can easily be removed from bones. Add raw vegetables to broth and simmer, uncovered until beans and potatoes are tender. Stir occasionally to prevent scorching. Add chicken, boned and diced, and seasonings. Note: If canned vegetables are used, include juices and reduce water to 2 quarts for thin stew, 1 quart for thick stew. Long slow cooking improves this stew.

SKYLINE DRIVE CORN CHOWDER

¾ cup onion, chopped
2 tablespoons butter or margarine
1 cup potatoes, peeled and diced
1 cup fully cooked ham, diced
2 cups fresh, frozen or canned sweet corn
1 cup cream-style corn
1 10-ounce can condensed cream of mushroom soup, undiluted
2½ cups milk
Salt and pepper to taste
1 tablespoon fresh parsley, chopped

In a heavy saucepan, cook the onion in butter until tender. Add all remaining ingredients; bring to a boil. Reduce heat; simmer, uncovered for 20-30 minutes.

PETRIFIED FOREST TOMATO SOUP

1 28-ounce can diced tomatoes, undrained
1 cup chicken broth
¼ cup butter or margarine
2 tablespoons sugar
1 tablespoon onion, chopped
⅛ teaspoon baking soda
2 cups heavy cream

In a saucepan, combine the first six ingredients. Cover and simmer for 1 hour. Heat cream in the top of a double boiler over simmering water; add to the tomato mixture just before serving: Serves: 8

FORD'S THEATRE BROCCOLI SOUP

2 packages frozen broccoli, chopped
¼ onion, chopped
2 cups chicken broth
2 tablespoons butter
1 tablespoon flour
1 teaspoon salt
⅛ teaspoon mace
Dash of pepper
2 cups light cream

Combine broccoli and onion to stock. Boil, then simmer 10 minutes. Put mixture through blender. Melt butter; add flour, salt, mace and pepper. Stir until smooth. Slowly stir in the cream, then broccoli mixture. American cheese can be added at final stage. Heat but do not boil.

BIG MEADOWS POTATO SOUP

4	cups potatoes, peeled and cubed
1	cup celery, chopped
1	cup onion, chopped
2	cups water
2	teaspoons salt
1	cup milk
1	cup whipping cream
1	tablespoon parsley flakes
⅛	teaspoon pepper
3	tablespoons butter

Combine potatoes, celery, onion, water and salt in large pot. Simmer, covered, about 20 minutes or until potatoes are tender. Mash potatoes a few times with masher. Stir in remaining ingredients; return to heat and cook but do not boil.

GUADALUPE GARDEN SOUP

½	pound mushrooms, quartered
3	onions, chopped
1	pound carrots, sliced
4	stalks celery, sliced
2	medium zucchini squash, sliced
1	box okra, sliced
1	28-ounce can tomatoes or juice
1	16-ounce can tomatoes
¼	teaspoon basil
¼	teaspoon pepper

Salt to taste

Microwave carrots a bit to soften. Combine all ingredients and simmer about 30 minutes so vegetables will still be rather crisp.

BRIGHT ANGEL BEEF STEW

3	slices bacon, cut in pieces
4	tablespoons flour
¼	teaspoon pepper
2	pounds lean beef, chunked
1	onion, chopped
2	garlic cloves, minced
1	28-ounce can tomato sauce
1	cup beef broth
1	cup dry red wine
1	bay leaf

Pinch thyme

4	carrots, sliced
2	celery stalks, sliced
12	mushrooms, sliced
4	large potatoes, peeled and quartered

In large pot, cook bacon. Combine flour, salt and pepper, and dredge beef. Brown in bacon grease. Add oil if needed. Add onion and garlic. Then add tomato sauce, broth, wine, and seasonings. Cover, cook slowly for 1 hour. Add carrots, celery, potatoes and mushrooms. Cook covered until vegetables are tender.

CADES COVE VEGETABLE BEEF SOUP

3	pounds beef cubes
1	8-ounce can tomato juice
⅓	cup onions, chopped
4	teaspoons salt
2	teaspoons Worcestershire sauce
¼	teaspoon chili powder
2	bay leaves
2	cups tomatoes
1	cup celery, diced
1	can corn
1	cup carrots, sliced
1	cup potatoes, diced
1	package frozen lima beans

Combine meat, tomato juice, onion, seasonings and 6 cups water in pot. Cover and simmer for 2 hours. Add vegetables; cover and simmer 1 hour. Serves: 8

DEVILS TOWER BEAN SOUP

1	pound navy beans
1½	pounds ham, cubed
2	quarts water
2	teaspoons salt
3	carrots, sliced
1	onion, diced
2	cups potatoes, diced
½	cup celery, chopped
½	cup green pepper, chopped
1	cup tomato juice
1	teaspoon sugar

Pepper to taste

Cook beans until almost tender. Add ham and remaining ingredients and simmer for one hour. Makes 3 quarts.

CAPE COD CLAM CHOWDER

1	large onion, diced
1	large potato, diced
1	can minced clams
1	quart milk
½	pint cream
1	teaspoon butter or margarine

Boil onion and potato in 1 cup salted water. Add clams; cook together for 5 minutes over low heat. Add milk and cream. Simmer over low heat. Add butter. Season to taste. Serves: 6

EL CAPITAN CIOPPIANO

1 green pepper, chopped
2 onions, chopped
1 clove garlic, minced
2 tablespoons oil
1 28-ounce can tomatoes, undrained
1 16-ounce can tomatoes, undrained
2 15-ounce cans tomato sauce
½ cup dry red wine
3 tablespoons snipped parsley
1 teaspoon salt
1 teaspoon dried oregano
½ teaspoon dried basil
Dash pepper
1 pound fish fillets, thawed and skinned
2½ pounds shrimp, cooked and deveined
2 6½-ounce cans minced clams

Brown green pepper, onions and garlic in oil until tender. Add tomatoes, tomato sauce, wine, parsley, salt, oregano, basil and pepper. Bring to a boil. Reduce heat. Cover and simmer 2 hours. Add fish fillets and simmer 10 minutes. Add shrimp that has been cut in large pieces. Simmer 10 minutes. Add clams, simmer 3 to 4 minutes.

JENNY LAKE RASPBERRY SOUP

2 cups frozen raspberries
½ cup sugar
½ cup sour cream
2 cups cold water
½ cup red wine

Puree raspberries in food processor or blender. Combine with remaining ingredients and chill. Serves: 4-6

SUNRISE PEACH SOUP

5 large, fully ripe peaches, peeled and quartered
¼ cup sugar (or more if needed)
1 cup sour cream
¼ cup fresh lemon juice
¼ cup white wine
1 tablespoon orange juice concentrate
Sliced peeled fresh peaches for garnish

Puree peaches and sugar in blender. Mix in sour cream. Add lemon juice, wine and orange juice and blend until smooth. Refrigerate until well chilled. Serves: 6-8

NATIONAL CAPITAL PARKS--
WASHINGTON, D. C.

The United States has in the District of Columbia a capital city that is as beautiful as can be found. It is complete with carefully landscaped parks, monuments, memorials, statues, parkways, buildings, streets and numerous other sites of commemoration--and each is a history lesson.

The White House was the capital's first public building. Its cornerstone was laid on October 13, 1792. Other very recognizable landmarks include the Washington Monument, the Jefferson Memorial, the Lincoln Memorial and the United States Capitol. In any trip to Washington, D.C., all of these sites should definitely be visited.

The Washington Monument, the 555' slender obelisk memorial in honor of our first president, George Washington, is easily found. Its observation landing at the top affords a bird's eye view of all of Washington. The Jefferson Memorial, a circular colonnaded structure commemorating President Thomas Jefferson, who drafted the Declaration of Independence, is south along the Tidal Basin. The Lincoln Memorial honoring President Abraham Lincoln, which holds his marble sitting statue and an inscription of his famous Gettysburg Address, is west along the Potomac River. The Capitol, where The Congress makes the Federal laws of our country, is east. Each is every bit worth the time and effort to visit. Also rewarding are the nearly 800 other sites however small or secluded each may be. Every person visiting Washington, D.C. will benefit from the experience. If you have not been to our nation's capital, put it in your plans to do so.

WASHINGTON MONUMENT

Golden Gate National Recreation Area, CA includes ocean beaches, a redwood forest, marshes, a cultural center and the famous Alcatraz Island in the San Francisco area.

On May 10, 1869 opposing eastern and western rail companies, Central Pacific Jupiter and Union Pacific 119 met at *Golden Spike National Historic Site*, UT completing the first transcontinental railroad in the United States.

The Grand *Coulee Dam National Recreation Area, WA* captures the Columbia River's waters and converts them into energy and recreation.

The impressive peaks of the Teton Range, stand 7,000 feet above the valley floor at *Grand Teton National Park*, WY. The Teton's clear lakes, abundant wildlife and picture postcard scenery make for an unforgettable adventure.

Grant-Kohrs Ranch National Historic Site, MT gives a glimpse of life on a 19th century ranch where great herds of cattle grazed before being driven to market.

The Lehman Caves in the *Great Basin National Park*, NV consist of winding tunnels connected to large vaulted rooms.

The dunes of *Great Sand Dunes National Monument*, CO are among the highest in the United States. Visits at dusk will find animals emerging from the sand to search for food.

McKittrick Canyon in *Guadalupe Mountains National Park*, TX has been called "the most beautiful spot in Texas." The park is a hiker's paradise.

The battle fought at *Guilford Courthouse National Military Park*, NC opened the campaign that led to the surrender of the British at Yorktown, VA in 1781.

Gulf Islands National Seashore, FL has brilliant white sand beaches, historic forts and nature trails all accessible by car.

Harpers Ferry National Historical Park, WV exchanged hands eight times during the Civil War. John Brown's historical raid took place here in 1859.

Harry S Truman National Historic Site, MO was the home of President Truman from 1919 until his death in 1972. Mrs. Truman's grandfather built the house known as the "Summer White House."

Take the Crater Rim road in *Hawaii Volcanoes National Park*, HI to see huge craters and numerous lava flows. A rain forest features Hawaiian tree ferns. The active Kilauea Iki volcano adds to this Hawaiian island.

Herbert Hoover National Historic Site, IA features the president's birthplace, boyhood neighborhood, the Presidential Library and Museum, and gravesite of the President and Mrs. Hoover.

CARLSBAD CAVERNS NATIONAL PARK

67

Homestead National Monument, NE commemorates the early settlers who came to this land to claim their 160 acres granted by the Homestead Act of 1862.

Future President Andrew Jackson directed a victorious assault at *Horseshoe Bend National Military Park*, AL in 1814 against Upper Creek warriors.

Hot Springs National Park, AR has been a favorite national spa for many years. The hot springs flow nearly a million gallons a day, and the temperature remains 143 degrees year-round. Elegant Bathhouse Row remains to envision the spa lifestyle and bathing industry of the 1920-1960's. The restored Fordyce Bathhouse, the grandest on the Row, is the park's visitor center and museum.

Hubbell Trading Post National Historic Site, AZ established in 1878, is still an active Navajo Indian trading post.

Independence Hall, *Independence National Historical Park*, PA is one of the most historically significant buildings in America. It was here that the Declaration of Independence was voted and proclaimed, General George Washington chosen for command of the armies, and the Constitution adopted. Visit the Liberty Bell and almost feel Benjamin Franklin's ghost looking over your shoulder.

The dunes at *Indiana Dunes National Lakeshore*, IN rise 180 feet above Lake Michigan's shore.

Truly a wilderness island, *Isle Royale National Park*, MI can be reached by boat in 2 to 6 hours, depending on the starting point. Bright blue lakes and sparkling rivers surrounded by rich green forests make up this island splendor.

A visit to New Orleans must include a stop at *Jean Lafitte National Historical Park*, LA. The Cajun culture, trails, canoe tours and jazz music are just a few interesting features of the park.

Jewel Cave National Monument, SD, has a cave system of chambers and passageways over 82 miles long.

John Fitzgerald Kennedy National Historic Site, MA is the birthplace and early boyhood home of the 35th President.

Touring the *John Muir National Historic Site*, CA adobe home, an excellent example of early California architecture, allows reflections on this world renown conservationist.

A break in the South Fork Dam in 1889 caused flooding of Johnstown, which now has the *Johnstown Flood National Memorial*, PA. The flood caused 2,209 deaths.

Vegetables

TWICE BAKED POTATOES

6   baking potatoes
1   teaspoon salt
¼   teaspoon pepper
¼   cup butter
½   cup sour cream
1   cup shredded Cheddar cheese
1   to 2 tablespoons chives, chopped
Bacon bits, if desired

Bake potatoes 60 minutes at 400 degrees or until done. Cut tops off and scoop potatoes out of shell and mash. Add ingredients and beat until fluffy. Spoon back into shells. Bake until hot or freeze until later; defrost then bake.

PETROGLYPH POTATO PANCAKES

4   medium potatoes
1   medium onion
1   egg, lightly beaten
1   teaspoon salt
¼   teaspoon white pepper
½   teaspoon baking soda
Dash nutmeg, if desired
Butter as needed

Wash and peel potatoes. Drop them in cold water for one hour or overnight. Grate potatoes fine and press to squeeze out excess liquid. Grate onion into potatoes. Add egg, seasonings and soda. Mix well. Heat 1½ tablespoons butter in large skillet. Drop a spoonful for each pancake, not too thick. Brown lightly, turn and brown other side. Drain. Serves: 4

GETTYSBURG POTATOES

4   baking potatoes
2   tablespoons butter
2   teaspoons paprika
1   teaspoon salt
½   teaspoon pepper

Peel potatoes and cut into large chunks; place in a shallow 2-quart baking pan. Pour melted butter over and stir until well coated. Sprinkle with paprika, salt and pepper. Bake uncovered at 350 degrees for 50 minutes or until potatoes are tender. Serves: 4

MOUNT RAINIER POTATOES

¾ cup onions, chopped
1 2-pound package frozen hash brown potatoes, thawed
1 16-ounce carton sour cream
1 can cream of celery soup
1½ cup Cheddar cheese, shredded
¼ cup butter, softened
1 teaspoon salt
1 teaspoon black pepper
½ cup round cracker crumbs

Combine first 8 ingredients; pour into greased 9x13-inch baking dish. Sprinkle cracker crumbs over top. Bake at 350 degrees for 40 minutes or until bubbly. Serves: 12

ARCHES POTATO CASSEROLE

12 potatoes, cooked and mashed
1 8-ounce package cream cheese
1 cup sour cream
Butter
Salt and pepper to taste
Onion salt or chives to taste

Mash potatoes while hot; add cream cheese, sour cream, butter and seasonings. Whip until smooth. Pour into greased 9x13-inch pan and sprinkle with Cheddar cheese or Parmesan cheese before baking at 350 degrees for 20 minutes. Serves: 12

RICHMOND FRIED SWEET POTATOES

Parboil for 15 minutes, 4 good sized sweet potatoes and remove skins. Cut thick slices lengthwise.

Fry in butter or oil. Serve with maple syrup.

FREDERICKSBURG SWEET POTATOES

3   cups sweet potatoes, mashed
2   eggs
1   cup granulated sugar
1   tablespoon vanilla
½   cup butter, melted
Topping:
1   cup nuts, chopped
1   cup brown sugar
5   tablespoons butter
⅓   cup flour

Mix sweet potatoes, eggs, sugar, vanilla and butter; put in greased baking dish. Mix topping ingredients together. Sprinkle on top of potatoes. Bake at 350 degrees for 25 minutes. Serves: 6

VICKSBURG BLACK-EYED PEAS

1   pound black-eyed peas
½   pound bacon, cooked and crumbled
1   large onion, chopped
1   garlic clove, minced
1   tablespoon butter
½   teaspoon thyme
Salt to taste

Place peas, bacon and enough water to cover in a large kettle; bring to boil. Boil for 3 minutes. Remove from heat; cover and let stand 1 hour. Do not drain. In a skillet, saute' onion and garlic in butter until tender. Add to pea mixture with thyme and salt. Return to heat; simmer, covered for 30 minutes or until peas are soft. Serves: 8

DEATH VALLEY ONION RINGS

1½ cups flour
1½ cups beer
3   large Bermuda onions
Oil

Sift flour into a plastic bowl. Gradually stir beer into flour. Cover and let mixture set for 3 hours at room temperature. Coat each onion ring with batter and fry in hot oil until crisp. To keep warm, place in 200 degree oven on heavy brown paper.

HOMESTEAD CORN MEDLEY

2   cups sweet corn
2   tablespoons butter
¼   cup onion, chopped
¼   cup green pepper, chopped
½   teaspoon salt
¼   teaspoon ground cumin
1   large tomato, chopped
2   tablespoons sugar

Combine first 6 ingredients in saucepan; cook and stir until butter is melted. Cover and cook over low heat for 10 minutes. Stir in tomato and sugar; cook covered 5 minutes.

BIG THICKET CORN

2½ pound package frozen corn
1   teaspoon salt
3   teaspoons sugar
¾   cup whipping cream
2   teaspoons cornstarch

Cook corn in a small amount of water. Add salt, sugar and cream. Bring to a boil and thicken with mixture of cornstarch and a little cream. Serves: 20

COULEE DAM CORN PUDDING

3   eggs, slightly beaten
1   16-ounce can whole kernel corn, drained
1   16-ounce can cream style corn
¾   cup milk
¼   cup butter, melted
1   teaspoon salt
Dash pepper
Swiss cheese slices

Pour half of combined mixture in buttered 8x8-inch baking pan. Place slices of cheese over layer; add remaining corn mixture. Sprinkle with paprika. Bake at 325 degrees for 45 minutes or until set.

NEW RIVER CROCKPOT CORN

20 ounces whole kernel corn
2 tablespoons sugar
8 ounces cream cheese, cubed
4 tablespoons margarine
6 tablespoons water

Combine all ingredients in crockpot and cook 4 hours on low setting. Serves: 6

SAGUARO POSOLE

2 cans hominy
1 can diced green chiles
1 cup Cheddar cheese, finely shredded
1 pint sour cream

Mix all ingredients well and heat in microwave on high for 8 minutes.

SCOTTS BLUFF CANDIED SQUASH

1 1-pound acorn or butternut squash
1 tablespoon brown sugar
1 tablespoon maple syrup or maple flavored syrup
1 tablespoon margarine or butter, melted
Dash ground nutmeg

Halve squash lengthwise. Scoop out seeds and discard. Arrange squash halves in a little water, upside down in a 2-quart square microwave baking dish. Cover with plastic wrap, turn back one corner to vent. Cook on high for 9 minutes or until tender. Drain. Mix brown sugar, syrup, margarine and nutmeg. Slice squash halves crosswise. Arrange in dish and pour syrup mixture over squash. Cook uncovered on high for 60 seconds more. Serves: 4 side dishes

ORGAN PIPE CHILI SQUASH

6   medium squash, quartered
1   cup sharp cheese, grated
1   4-ounce can green chilis, chopped
½   cup bread crumbs

Cook squash until almost tender. Drain and add cheese and chilis. Pour into buttered casserole and top with bread crumbs. Bake at 350 degrees for 30 minutes. Serves: 6

ZUCCHINI BOATS

8   to 10 medium zucchini
½   cup butter
1   cup Cheddar cheese, grated
1   cup sour cream
½   teaspoon salt
¼   cup onion, minced
1   cup buttered bread crumbs
Parmesan cheese

Use unpeeled zucchini. Cut in half and boil until almost tender, about 10 minutes. Transfer drained zucchini to 9x12-inch baking dish. Melt butter; mix in cheese, sour cream, salt and onion. Pour over zucchini, dot with butter and sprinkle with Parmesan cheese and bread crumbs. Bake at 350 degrees for 20-25 minutes. Serves: 8

STATUE OF LIBERTY EGGPLANT

2   small eggplants, cut in ½-inch slices
2   tablespoons oil
1   packet Italian herb mixture
1   15-ounce can tomato sauce
Minced parsley
6   cloves garlic, minced
¼   cup cooking wine
10 ounces Mozzarella cheese, sliced

Marinate 4 of the minced garlic cloves overnight in the tomato sauce, herb mixture and wine. Oil a medium size casserole and layer the eggplant; sprinkle with remaining 2 minced garlic cloves. Pour ¾ of the tomato mixture over eggplant and layer cheese on top. Add remaining tomato mixture. Sprinkle with minced parsley. Bake at 350 degrees for 45 minutes. Serves: 4

EVERGLADES GREEN BEANS

1	small can water chestnuts, sliced
1	small can mushrooms, sliced; save juice
⅓	cup onion, chopped
3	cans (No.2) French style green beans, drained

Sauce:

4	tablespoons butter
⅓	cup flour
⅓	cup milk
½	cup American cheese
1	teaspoon soy sauce
⅛	teaspoon salt
¼	teaspoon hot pepper sauce

Saute' water chestnuts, mushrooms and onion in 2 tablespoons butter. Add mixture to green beans in large casserole dish. To make sauce: melt butter, add flour, then slowly add milk, stirring to thicken. Add cheese, soy sauce, salt and pepper sauce. Put layer of green beans mixture; then cheese sauce, layer of green beans, etc. into casserole. Bake in 325 degree oven for 45 minutes or until bubbly. Serves: 12-15

BROCCOLI SUPREME

2	packages frozen chopped broccoli
2	eggs
2	cans mushroom soup
1	cup mayonnaise
1	medium onion, chopped
1	cup Pepperidge Farm stuffing
½	cup butter, melted
½	to ¾ cup shredded Cheddar cheese

Cook broccoli and drain well. In bowl beat eggs; add soup, mayonnaise and onion. Add broccoli. Pour into buttered 2-quart casserole. Add cheese. Top with stuffing. Pour melted butter over all. Bake at 350 degrees for about 45 minutes.

LEMON BROCCOLI

1	small bunch broccoli
2	tablespoons butter

Juice of half a lemon
Salt to taste
Freshly ground pepper to taste

Cut and trim broccoli into flowerets. Bring enough water to boil to cover broccoli. Add salt to taste and add broccoli. Cook briefly, about 3 to 4 minutes or until crisp tender. Drain well. Heat butter in saucepan and add lemon juice. Pour this over the broccoli. Sprinkle with salt and pepper to taste. Serves: 4

SHILOH SAUTEED OKRA

Okra, fresh or frozen
Salt and pepper to taste
Seasonings to taste: cayenne pepper,
    blackened, garlic salt, seasoning
    salt, etc.

Cut ends off okra. Melt a little butter in skillet. Drop in okra and stir fry with seasonings until okra is tender. Serve immediately.

CHILI SAUCE

24 medium size ripe tomatoes
4   white onions
3   sweet peppers
2   cups sugar
2   cups vinegar
2   tablespoons salt
½   teaspoon allspice
½   teaspoon cloves
1   tablespoon cinnamon

Peel the tomatoes and clean the onions and run with the peppers through a food chopper. Then add all the other ingredients and cook for at least 2 hours. Thicken to the desired consistency of flour paste. Seal in sterilized jars or use immediately.

ZION VEGETABLE RELISH

5   medium tomatoes, peeled and
    diced
1   medium green pepper, diced
1   small onion, diced
½   cup celery, diced
⅓   cup water
2   tablespoons sugar
2   tablespoons white vinegar
1½ teaspoons salt
⅛   teaspoon pepper

Combine all ingredients in medium bowl; stir well. Cover and chill before serving. Yield: 3½ cups

RED BEANS AND RICE

1	pound dried red beans
1	quart hot water
1	large ham bone with meat
1	large onion, chopped
½	cup green onions, chopped
2	garlic cloves, minced
1	bay leaf
½	teaspoon cayenne pepper
1½	teaspoons salt
1	pound smoked link sausage, cut in one inch pieces

Hot cooked rice

Sort beans, rinse well. Cover beans with tap water and soak overnight. Drain beans, place in large pot; add hot water, ham bone, onion, green onion, garlic, bay leaf, cayenne and salt. Bring mixture to a boil; cover and reduce heat. Simmer beans 2 hours, or until tender, adding water if necessary. Stir often.
Add sausage to beans and simmer, uncovered about 15 minutes longer, or until a thick gravy forms. Stir occasionally. Serve over rice

GARLIC-CHEESE GRITS

1	cup grits, uncooked
1	package garlic cheese, shredded
¼	pound Cheddar cheese, shredded
1	stick oleo
3	dashes Worcestershire sauce
3	egg whites, stiffly beaten

Cook grits. Add cheeses, butter, and Worcestershire sauce. Set aside. Just before ready to bake, add or fold in egg whites. Bake 30 minutes in 350 degree oven.

FORT SMITH RICE PILAF

½ medium red onion, diced
½ red and yellow bell peppers, diced
2 green onions, thinly sliced
1 tablespoon each garlic and shallots
½ cup corn
Butter for sauteing
½ cup pecans, chopped
1½ cups each wild rice and long grain rice, cooked
Chicken broth
Butter

In a skillet, saute' the vegetables in butter; add the pecans and the rices. Add a little broth and butter. Season with salt and pepper.

WILD RICE CASSEROLE

⅓ cup butter or margarine
1 10¾-ounce can beef consomme
1 10¾-ounce can onion soup
1 8-ounce can water chestnuts, drained and sliced
1 8-ounce can mushrooms, drained and sliced
1 6-ounce box long grain and wild rice
1 scant soup can of water
½ cup long grain rice (white or brown)

Combine butter, beef consomme, and onion soup in a 1½-quart casserole. Place in 350 degree oven until butter melts. Add water chestnuts, mushrooms and rice with seasonings that are included in box. Stir to mix, return to oven and bake uncovered for one hour. Serves: 8

SANTA FE RICE, CHILI AND CHEESE

1 cup rice
2 cups sour cream
½ pound Cheddar or Monterey Jack cheese, grated
1 4-ounce can green chiles, chopped
Salt to taste
¼ cup Parmesan cheese, grated

Cook rice until just tender, do not overcook. Combine rice, sour cream, cheese and green chiles. Season to taste. Pour into a buttered 2-quart casserole. Dot with butter and sprinkle with Parmesan. Bake uncovered at 350 degrees for 30 minutes and serve immediately. May be prepared ahead and refrigerated. Allow to warm to room temperature before baking. Serves: 6-8

SWEET DILL PICKLES

1   quart whole dill pickles
2   cups granulated sugar

Drain all juice from pickles. Slice them cross wise, thick or thin. Put into large bowl, cover with sugar. No juice. Stir to mix well. Cover and let stand overnight until sugar melts. Pack in jar with juice. Refrigerate at least 3 days before eating.

ANTIETAM REFRIGERATOR CUCUMBERS

8   cups cucumbers, peeled and sliced
1   cup onions, sliced thinly
1   cup green peppers, cut up
2   tablespoons salt
1   cup vinegar
2   cups sugar
1   teaspoon mustard seed
1   teaspoon celery seed

Peel and slice cucumbers, onions and green peppers. Sprinkle 2 tablespoons salt on vegetables and set 1 hour in refrigerator. Meanwhile, mix vinegar, sugar, mustard seed, and celery seed until sugar is dissolved. (May microwave mixture; then cool.) Put a few ice cubes on top of vegetables and rinse well in a colander; drain. Place vegetables in 2 quart jars and pour vinegar mixture over and cover with lids. Place in refrigerator and use 3 days later. These keep well!

HOMEMADE PICKLES

2   pounds (about 10) pickling cucumbers
2   cups water
2   cups white vinegar
½   cup sugar
2   cloves of garlic, chopped
1   tablespoon coarse salt
2   tablespoons dill seed or fresh dill

In a large bowl, combine all ingredients. Cover and let stand at room temperature for one hour. Fit cucumbers, either whole or halved into 2 quart jars; pour on enough of vinegar mixture to cover and tighten lids. Refrigerate at least one week.

GREAT SMOKY MOUNTAINS NATIONAL PARK

Great Smoky Mountains National Park receives its name from the smokelike haze that covers its mountains and valleys. The haze is created by the vast amount of water vapor rising from the park's dense vegetation.

The park's mountains may not reach the heights of some mountains in other parks, but they are impressive in their own right. Several are over 6000 feet high and Clansman's Dome is the highest at 6643 feet. Where higher mountains in other parks may be treeless or have sparse vegetation, the Great Smoky Mountains are covered.

These special mountains, some of the oldest on Earth, have an origin beginning an estimated 500 million years ago. Various seas deposited their sediments, which were then subjected to long and slow land upheavals. The extent of the upheavals is interesting, especially when you visit the places where you see older rocks on top of younger rocks.

There is no other place of comparable size to the park in the Eastern United States having such a large number of plants. Noteworthy are the variety of hardwood trees, and at higher elevations, the red spruce.

This over one-half million acre park sits in the Appalachian Highlands on the boundary of two states -- North Carolina and Tennessee. It is filled with natural and cultural beauty all of its own. The major scenic drive is the Newfound Gap Road. It traverses the park north to south and draws bumper-to-bumper traffic during the summer and times of the autumn when visitors come to witness the incredible foliage colors.

The history of the early settlers is lovingly preserved in the park. Pioneer homes, churches, and farms allow visitors to step back in time to rural America at its best.

"SUGAR," OCONALUFTEE FARM

The Joshua tree is an overgrown member of the yucca family. Its arms reach out in all directions beckoning visitors to *Joshua Tree National Park*, CA.

Katmai National Park and Preserve, AK was initially recognized for its volcanic importance. The park contains the largest carnivore in the world—the Alaska brown bear.

The Army of Tennessee fortified *Kennesaw Mountain National Battlefield Park*, GA in its attempt to halt General Sherman from advancing to the Confederate's supply house in Atlanta.

The Martin Luther King, Jr. National Historic Site, GA contains the birthplace, church and grave of the famous civil rights leader.

When *Kings Canyon National Park*, CA and its giant sequoia trees were added to the National Park System, they were forever protected from logging.

Klondike Gold Rush National Historical Park, AK has historic buildings and trails of the gold rush era. A visitor center is located in Seattle, Washington.

Lake Mead National Recreation Area, NV has Lake Mead formed by Hoover Dam and Lake Mojave formed by Davis Dam. Surrounded by desert country it is America's first national recreation area.

Lake Meredith National Recreation Area, TX is a manmade lake very popular with outdoor recreation enthusiasts in the Texas panhandle.

Lassen Peak Volcano erupted at various times between 1914 and 1921. *Lassen Volcanic National Park*, CA has other geothermal features which can still be seen today.

The lava beds of *Lava Beds National Monument*, CA create an incredible landscape. The connecting lava cave to the visitor center shows an inner example of the park.

Nancy Hanks, President Abraham Lincoln's mother is buried at *Lincoln Boyhood National Memorial*, IN.

Abraham Lincoln resided in his home at *Lincoln Home National Historic Site*, IL for seventeen years before becoming president. The surrounding historic homes give visitors a nostalgic trip back to Lincoln's time.

Lt. Col. George Custer and all men of five companies lost their lives at *Little Bighorn Battlefield National Monument*, MT when the U.S. Cavalry, Sioux and Northern Cheyenne Indians battled on June 25-26, 1876.

At Henry Wadsworth *Longfellow National Historic Site*, MA the poet lived in his mansion from 1837 to 1882 which was close to Harvard where he taught.

Lowell National Historical Park, MA tells a story of labor history with its Boott Cotton Mills Museum, the Suffolk Mill turbine, and textile mills.

The 36th president's birthplace, boyhood home, and ranch make up the *Lyndon B. Johnson National Historical Park*, TX.

Mammoth Cave National Park, KY is the longest recorded cave system in the world with 336 miles of explored and mapped areas.

Confederate Brig. Gen. Thomas J. Jackson acquired his nickname "Stonewall" at the battle of Manassas, *Manassas National Battlefield Park*, VA.

The pre-Columbian cliff dwellings at *Mesa Verde National Park*, CO are some of the nation's most famous and best preserved. As many as forty pueblos and cliff dwellings are visible from park roads.

Minute Man National Historical Park, MA is the scene of the fighting on April 19, 1775, when farmers and merchants took up arms against their mother country, England, to defend their adopted land. Their first shots started the American Revolution.

MOUNT RUSHMORE NATIONAL MEMORIAL

The stand of giant redwoods at *Muir Woods National Monument*, CA was named for John Muir, writer and conservationist. Close to San Francisco, the park enables visitors to walk among the tall trees and feel close to nature.

Named after the Aztec leader Montezuma, *Montezuma Castle National Monument*, AZ is one of the best preserved cliff dwellings in the United States.

General George Washington and his Continental Army spent two of the coldest, most miserable winters of the campaign at *Morristown National Historical Park*, NJ.

The dormant, majestic volcano Mt. Rainier in *Mt. Rainier National Park*, WA is the tallest peak in the Cascade Range. Nearly three miles high, it can be seen from 100 miles away.

Truly a monumental piece of work is that of Gutzon Borglum at *Mt. Rushmore National Memorial*, SD. The faces of President's George Washington, Thomas Jefferson, Theodore Roosevelt and Abraham Lincoln are carved on a granite mountain. The park is most impressive.

The *Natchez Trace Parkway* is a 445 mile scenic highway, following the historic trails of Indians and traders between Nashville, Tennessee and Natchez, Mississippi.

Kayenta Anasazi Indians have constructed interesting cliff dwellings at *Navajo National Monument*, AZ .

New River Gorge National River, WV is among the oldest rivers on the continent.

Nez Perce National Historical Park, ID interprets and protects the history of the Nez Perce Indians.

Sometimes called the "American Alps," *North Cascades National Park*, WA preserves lush forests, meadows and hundreds of glaciers. Hikers, mountaineers and backpackers are attracted to the park in record numbers. "Cascade Loop" drive through the park is most spectacular.

Ocmulgee National Monument, GA includes temple mounds of Mississippian Indian culture in 1000 AD.

Olympic National Park, WA is highly diversified in character and climate. It has mountains, glaciers, seacoast, rain forests and unbelievable weather changes. Its rain forests have vegetation as luxurious as the Amazon Jungle. Many hikers say this park is one of the best to hike.

Carved out of a marble mountain, *Oregon Caves National Monument*, OR has many unusual formations.

Breads

GRIZZLY BEAR PANCAKES

1¼ cups flour, sifted
3 teaspoons baking powder
1 tablespoon sugar
½ teaspoon salt
1 egg, beaten
1 cup milk
2 tablespoons oil

Sift together flour, baking powder, sugar and salt. Combine egg, milk, and oil; add to dry ingredients, stirring just till flour is moistened. Bake on hot griddle. Makes eight 4-inch pancakes.

SOUTH RIM BUTTERMILK PANCAKES

2 eggs, beaten with hand mixer until fluffy
2 cups flour
2 teaspoons baking powder
1 teaspoon salt
2 cups buttermilk
1 teaspoon soda
2 tablespoons sugar
4 tablespoons oil

Beat 2 eggs with hand mixer until fluffy. Beat in remaining ingredients. Oil the griddle for these flapjacks. Makes eight 4-inch pancakes.

LOGAN PASS BUTTERMILK WAFFLES

1¾ cups sifted flour or 2 cups cake flour
2 teaspoons baking powder
½ teaspoon salt
½ teaspoon baking soda
2 egg yolks, beaten
1¼ cups buttermilk
½ cup oil
2 egg whites, stiffly beaten

Sift together dry ingredients. Combine egg yolks and milk; stir into dry ingredients. Stir in oil. Fold in egg whites, leaving a few fluffs. Bake in preheated waffle baker. Makes about 8 waffles.

MIRROR LAKE
BLUEBERRY BUTTERMILK MUFFINS

2	cups all-purpose flour
½	cup sugar
2¼	teaspoons baking powder
1	teaspoon salt
¼	teaspoon soda
1	egg
1	cup buttermilk
¼	cup butter, melted
1	cup blueberries

Combine dry ingredients in mixing bowl; set aside. Combine egg, buttermilk and butter; mix well. Make well in dry ingredients. Pour in liquid ingredients and stir just to moisten. Fold in blueberries. Fill muffin pans ⅔ full. Bake at 425 degrees for 20-25 minutes.

WIND CAVE WHEAT BREAD

2	cups whole wheat flour
1	teaspoon baking powder
1	teaspoon baking soda
1	teaspoon salt
1	egg
2	cups buttermilk
1½	tablespoons butter, melted
½	cup walnuts, chopped
3	tablespoons light molasses or honey
½	cup seedless raisins

Grease 9x5-inch loaf pan. Heat oven to 400 degrees. Mix flour, baking powder, soda and salt. Beat egg in large bowl. Stir in buttermilk, molasses (or honey) and butter. Stir in flour mixture. Mix in walnuts and raisins. Place batter into loaf pan and bake 50-60 minutes or until bread is well browned on top. Remove from oven and place on wire racks to cool.

CAVE ISLAND RASPBERRY BUTTER

1	10-ounce package frozen raspberries, thawed and drained
1	cup butter
2	cups powdered sugar

Soften butter and cream with sugar. Add thawed and drained raspberries. Mix until smooth. Great on pancakes or muffins.

KAIBAB JALAPEÑO CHEESE ROLLS

1   package crescent rolls, any brand
1   cup medium Cheddar cheese, grated
1   jar pickled jalapeño slices, drained

In the center of each roll, place 3 jalapeño slices. Top with cheese. Roll dough and bake according to package directions.

RIO GRANDE CHILE BREAD

1   loaf Italian or French bread, unsliced
1   stick butter, melted
1   4-ounce can green chiles, diced and drained
½   cup cheese, grated

Slice bread almost all the way through. Combine melted butter, chiles and cheese; spread between bread slices. Place loaf on plate and cover with paper towel. Microwave on 50% power until cheese melts.

YAVAPAI CHILE CHEESE PUPPIES

4   cups vegetable oil
¾   cup all purpose flour
¾   cornmeal
2   teaspoons baking powder
1   teaspoon garlic salt
¼   teaspoon cayenne pepper
1   cup shredded Cheddar cheese
1   4-ounce can diced green chiles
½   cup minced fresh onion
¼   cup chopped green onion
¼   cup milk
1   egg, beaten
Guacamole dip

In deep heavy-bottom saucepan, heat oil to 350 degrees. In large bowl, combine flour, cornmeal, baking powder, garlic salt and cayenne pepper. In small bowl, mix together remaining ingredients except guacamole. Stir cheese mixture into flour mixture until all ingredients are moistened; let stand 5 minutes. Drop by scant tablespoonfuls into hot oil. Fry 3 to 4 minutes, until golden brown, turning as needed. Drain on paper towels. Serve with guacamole. Makes about 36 hush puppies.

ST. LOUIS MONKEY BREAD

2   packages yeast
2   cups warm water
¾   cup oil
¾   cup sugar
1½ teaspoons salt
3   eggs
7   cups bread flour
2   sticks margarine, melted

Dissolve yeast in water; add sugar, salt, oil, eggs and 3½ cups flour. Beat well and add rest of flour until dough is soft. Let rise 2 hours or until double in size. Roll out dough on lightly floured board to ¼-inch thickness. Cut dough in 2½-inch long pieces. Dip each piece in melted butter and arrange in layers in buttered bundt pan. Let rise until almost doubled in bulk. Bake at 350 degrees for 30 to 40 minutes, or until golden brown. Freezes well and can be reheated. To serve, invert pan on platter; pieces pull apart easily.

LIBERTY BELL SELF-RISING ROLLS

1   package yeast
1   egg, beaten
1½ sticks butter, melted
2   cups warm water
¼   cup sugar
4   cups self-rising flour

Dissolve yeast in warm water. Melt butter and cream with sugar. Add beaten egg. Stir in yeast. Add flour and mix well. Drop by spoonfuls into well greased muffin tins. Bake at 375 degrees for 20 to 25 minutes. Dough can be refrigerated for several days.

CUMBERLAND GAP SPOONBREAD

1   cup white cornmeal
3   cups milk
1   teaspoon salt
1   teaspoon baking powder
2   tablespoons butter, melted
3   eggs, separated

Cook cornmeal and 2 cups milk until stiff, about 8 minutes. Stir frequently, remove from heat. Add salt, baking powder, melted butter and remaining 1 cup milk. Beat egg yolks well and add to cornmeal mixture. Beat egg whites until stiff and fold in carefully. Bake in greased 2-quart casserole in 375 degree oven for 40 minutes or until brown on top. Spoon out and serve with butter.

GRAND LAKE COFFEE CAN BREAD

4	cups all-purpose flour
1	package dry yeast
½	cup butter
½	cup water
½	cup milk
¼	cup sugar
1	teaspoon salt
2	eggs, slightly beaten
½	cup chopped nuts, (optional)
½	cup chopped raisins, (optional)

Coat insides of two 1-pound coffee cans with small amounts of cooking oil. In a large bowl, mix 2 cups flour and yeast together. In a saucepan, stir together butter, water, milk, sugar and salt over low heat until butter melts. Cool 5 minutes. Add to flour and yeast. Mix in 2 more cups flour, eggs, nuts and raisins. Dough will be stiff. Turn onto a floured board; knead until dough is smooth and elastic. Divide dough in half; place in prepared coffee cans. Cover with plastic lids and let rise in warm place until dough is 1-inch from the top. Preheat oven to 375 degrees. Remove plastic lids and bake 35 minutes. Remove from cans and cool. Makes 2 loaves.

NEW ORLEANS BEIGNETS

1	cup boiling water
2	tablespoons unsalted butter
¼	cup sugar
¼	teaspoon salt
½	cup evaporated milk
½	package active dry yeast (2 teaspoons)
1	beaten egg
3	cups all-purpose flour
Vegetable oil for frying	
Confectioner's sugar	

In mixer bowl, combine boiling water, butter, salt, sugar, milk, yeast and egg. Slowly mix in flour and combine until you have a dough. Roll to ⅛-inch thickness and cut into 2-inch squares. Do not allow dough to rise. Heat oil to 375 degrees and fry squares until golden brown. Serve with a light dusting of confectioners' sugar.

SUGARLANDS BREAKFAST PULLAPART

1	cup chopped pecans
⅔	cup sugar
2	to 3 teaspoons ground cinnamon
1	(1-pound) loaf frozen bread dough, thawed
6	tablespoons butter or margarine, melted

Sprinkle pecans in bottom of a lightly greased 9-inch pieplate. Set aside. Mix sugar and cinnamon; set aside. Cut bread into quarters; cut each quarter into 6 pieces. Dip each piece in butter; coat in sugar mixture. Place dough pieces over pecans. Cover; let rise in warm place (85 degrees) free from drafts for 1 hour. Bake at 350 degrees 30 minutes or until done. Immediately invert on serving plate.

GLACIER HEATH BRICKLE COFFEE CAKE

¼ pound butter
2 cups flour
1 cup brown sugar
½ cup white sugar
1 cup buttermilk
1 teaspoon soda
1 egg
1 teaspoon vanilla
½ cup Heath Brickle
Topping:
½ cup Heath Brickle
½ cup pecans, chopped

Blend flour, butter and sugars together. Take out ½ cup of the mixture. To the remaining add buttermilk, soda, egg, vanilla and ½ cup Heath Brickle. Blend well. Pour into greased and floured 10x14x2-inch cake pan. Mix remaining Heath Brickle with ¼ cup chopped pecans and add to the ½ cup reserved flour, butter and sugar mixture. Sprinkle over the top of the batter and bake in a 350 degree oven for 30 minutes.

HALEAKALA SOUR CREAM COFFEE CAKE

1 cup butter, softened
2 cups sugar
2 eggs
1 cup sour cream
1 teaspoon vanilla
2 cups cake flour, sifted
1 teaspoon salt
1 teaspoon baking powder
½ cup pecans
2 teaspoons cinnamon
4 tablespoons brown sugar

Cream butter and sugar; add eggs 1 at a time, beating well after each addition. Fold in sour cream and vanilla. Sift flour, salt and baking powder; add to mixture. Pour half batter into greased and floured tube pan. Make topping by mixing pecans, cinnamon and brown sugar. Sprinkle on half the topping. Pour in remaining batter; sprinkle on remaining topping. Bake at 350 degrees for 55 to 60 minutes. Cool; remove from pan and sprinkle with brown sugar.

JACKSON HOLE BANANA BREAD

½ cup shortening
1 cup sugar
1 cup bananas
1 teaspoon soda
¼ teaspoon salt
2 eggs
2 cups sifted flour
1 teaspoon vanilla
½ cup nuts

Cream sugar and shortening. Add beaten eggs, then sifted dry ingredients alternately with bananas. Add nuts last. Spoon into greased and floured loaf pan. Bake in 350 degree oven for 40 or 50 minutes or until toothpick comes out clean.

BANDELIER EGGNOG BREAD

¼ cup butter or margarine, melted
¾ cup sugar
2 eggs, beaten
2¼ cups all-purpose flour
2 teaspoons baking powder
1 teaspoon salt
1 cup eggnog
½ cup chopped pecans
½ cup raisins
½ cup chopped red and green candied cherries

In a large bowl, combine butter, sugar and eggs; mix well. Combine flour, baking powder and salt. Stir into butter mixture alternately with eggnog; mix only until dry ingredients are moistened. Fold in pecans, raisins and cherries. Spoon into a greased 8½x4½x2½-inch loaf pan. Bake at 350 degrees for 70 minutes or until bread tests done. Yield: 1 loaf

CHEROKEE ORANGE DATE BREAD

1 cup butter or margarine, softened
2 cups sugar
3 eggs, beaten
4 cups all-purpose flour
1 teaspoon baking soda
1 teaspoon salt
1⅓ cups buttermilk
1 cup chopped walnuts
1 cup chopped dates
1 tablespoon grated orange peel
Glaze:
¼ cup orange juice
½ cup sugar
2 tablespoons orange peel, grated

In a mixing bowl, cream butter and sugar. Add eggs; mix well. Combine flour, baking soda and salt; add to creamed mixture alternately with buttermilk. Fold in walnuts, dates and orange peel. Pour into 2 greased and floured 8½x4½x2½-inch loaf pans. Bake at 350 degrees for 60 to 65 minutes or until done. Combine glaze ingredients; spoon half over hot bread. Cool for 10 minutes. Remove from pans; spoon remaining glaze over bread. Yield: 2 loaves

ALCATRAZ LEMON BREAD

½ cup butter
1 cup sugar
2 eggs, beaten
1½ cups flour
1 teaspoon baking powder
½ teaspoon salt
½ cup milk
1 cup chopped pecans
Grated rind of one lemon
Juice of one lemon
¼ cup sugar

Cream together butter and 1 cup of sugar. Stir in beaten eggs. Sift flour, baking powder and salt together. Add dry ingredients alternately with milk to the sugar-butter mixture. Add pecans and lemon rind. Pour into a greased and floured loaf pan. Bake at 350 degrees for 45 minutes to 1 hour. After bread is removed from oven, pierce top with a toothpick. Combine lemon juice and sugar. Pour over hot bread.

YOSEMITE NATIONAL PARK

Yosemite National Park, established in 1890, is the oldest and one of the best-known national parks in California. When first made a national park, Yosemite Valley, one of the most beautiful places in the West, and the Mariposa Grove, an outstanding collection of giant sequoia trees, were not included. This was because in 1864 the United States Government knowing their park value provided them to the State of California for state parks. In 1906, however, California returned the areas to the United States for inclusion in Yosemite National Park. These are "must see" places during any visit.

Yosemite is located in the Sierra Nevada Mountains about 200 miles east of San Francisco.

It is difficult to identify in a few words how land upheavals, water, ice and time have created this landscape masterpiece.

Major features catching every visitor's eye are Half Dome and El Capitan, which stand as pronounced granite sentries protecting the park. Equally impressive are the numerous waterfalls shooting off the high valley walls. Yosemite Falls is created as Yosemite Creek rolls out of its bed and into space for an almost one-half mile cascading drop to the valley floor. Others include Bridalveil, Vernal and Nevada. Although each fall is different and beautiful, when the melting winter snows increase their volume of water, they are even more spectacular.

The mountains, valleys, forests, meadows, lakes, streams, wildlife, trails and history of Yosemite make it a natural jewel in the crown of the national parks. This national park is definitely one where you should plan to park your vehicle and hike to experience its grandeur to the fullest.

YOSEMITE FALLS

Exploring the 134 miles of the Current and Jacks Fork Rivers at *Ozark National Scenic Riverways*, MO is a boater's dream.

Padre Island National Seashore, TX on the Gulf of Mexico has incredible sand beaches, excellent fishing and bird and marine life.

The first battle of the 1846-48 Mexican War took place at *Palo Alto Battlefield National Historic Site*, TX.

The Union Army experienced victory in the Civil War battle of March 7-8, 1862 at *Pea Ridge National Military Park*, AR.

Pecos National Historical Park, NM preserves the ruins of the large Pecos Pueblo, a major trade center, and ruins of two Spanish 17th and 18th century colonial missions.

A ten month campaign in 1864-1865 was waged by the Union Army to seize Petersburg of *Petersburg National Battlefield*, VA.

See petrified trees, Indian ruins and petroglyphs, and part of the Painted Desert at *Petrified Forest National Park*, AZ.

Beautiful sandstone cliffs resembling castles give *Pictured Rocks National Lakeshore*, MI, the first national lakeshore, its name.

The spires, domes and caves of *Pinnacles National Monument*, CA are worth visiting. The spirelike formations rise from six hundred to a thousand feet from the floor of the canyon, visible for miles in every direction.

Point Reyes National Seashore, CA peninsula has long beaches, tall cliffs and offshore bird and sea lion colonies for anyone interested in the differing observations of a California coastal area.

Richmond National Battlefield Park, VA commemorates several Civil War battles to capture Richmond, the Confederate capitol.

Redwood National Park, CA offers scenic Pacific coastline and colossal redwood forests. To walk among the giant redwood trees is an unforgettable forest adventure.

Only two hours from Denver, *Rocky Mountain National Park*, CO is one of the most visited high country parks in the United States. Trail Ridge Road, which crosses the Continental Divide allows a breathtaking view of the Rocky Mountains, with some peaks over 14,000 feet high.

Val-Kill Cottage at *Eleanor Roosevelt National Historic Site*, NY was used by Mrs. Roosevelt as a personal retreat.

Theodore Roosevelt National Park, ND was established April 25, 1947. The park is known for the scenic badlands and the former president's Elkhorn Ranch.

Russell Cave National Monument, AL in northeast Alabama, is a cave recording human habitation from 7000 BC to 1650 AD.

The beautiful Saint Croix River of *Saint Croix National Scenic Riverway*, WI begins in the wilds of northern Wisconsin and flows 252 miles to the great Mississippi River.

Visit *Franklin D. Roosevelt's home*, Springwood in Hyde Park; *Martin Van Buren's home*, Lindenwald in Kinderhook; and *Theodore Roosevelt's home*, Sagamore Hill in Oyster Bay. All are in New York.

See giant saguaro cacti, sometimes 50 feet tall in the cactus forest of *Saguaro National Park*, AZ.

HOT SPRINGS NATIONAL PARK

Salem Maritime National Historic Site, MA uses historic buildings and interpretive programs to tell the story of Salem's past bustling maritime life.

Four Spanish frontier missions which exhibit an interesting part of Spanish colonization in the southwest are the focal point of *San Antonio Missions National Historical Park*, TX .

The Castillo San Felipe del Morro at *San Juan National Historic Site*, PR is the second largest Spanish fort built in the new world.

Santa Monica Mountains National Recreation Area, CA is typical west coast environment living: rugged landscape, terrific weather and colors of every hue.

The American victory over the British in 1777 at *Saratoga National Historical Park*, NY was the turning point of the Revolution.

Groves of giant Sequoias are an absolute wonder in the High Sierra of *Sequoia National Park*, CA. A visit to General Sherman, the largest tree, is a highlight of a Sequoia visit.

Shenandoah National Park is located in the Blue Ridge Mountains of Virginia. Skyline Drive, a winding 105 mile road along the crest of the Blue Ridge, provides breathtaking overlook views.

On April 6, 1862 the surprised Union troops were attacked by the Confederate army, but one day later responded and reclaimed their lost ground at *Shiloh National Military Park*, TN.

The large colorful totem poles at *Sitka National Historical Park*, AK are the work of the Tlingit Indians.

Sleeping Bear Dunes National Lakeshore, MI along Lake Michigan shores contains dunes, lakes, islands and beaches.

Steamtown National Historical Site, PA in downtown Scranton interprets the story of the early 20th century steam railroad period in America.

Just outside of Flagstaff, AZ visitors can see sandstone pueblo ruins of 1000 AD at *Wupatki National Monument*, cliff dwellings built in caves about 1200 AD at *Walnut Canyon National Monument*, and an extinct volcano at *Sunset Crater Volcano National Monument*, AZ.

The colorful limestone caves at *Timpanogos Cave National Monument*, UT are noted for helictite formations.

In 1864, Confederate Lt. General Nathan Bedford Forrest tried to cut the railroad supplying the Union's march on Atlanta at *Tupelo National Battlefield*, MS.

Desserts

LINCOLN APPLE PIE

7   tart apples
1   cup sugar
2   tablespoons flour
1   teaspoon cinnamon
Dash nutmeg
Dash salt
Pastry for 2 crust pie
2   tablespoons butter

Pare apples and slice thin. Combine sugar, flour, spices and salt; mix with apples. Line 9-inch pie plate with pastry, fill with apple mixture; dot with butter. Adjust top crust; sprinkle with sugar for sparkle. Bake in 400 degree oven for 50 minutes.

SITKA COCONUT CREAM PIE

2   pie shells, baked
4   ounces cream cheese, softened
¼   cup sugar
1   package non-dairy topping mix
½   cup milk
1   teaspoon vanilla
1   cup shredded coconut
2   3-ounce packages instant vanilla
    pie mix
1   teaspoon vanilla
1   cup coconut, toasted
Whipped cream

Combine cream cheese, sugar, topping mix, milk and vanilla. Beat until light and fluffy. Pour into pie shells. Spread ½ cup coconut on each pie and chill several hours. Prepare instant pie filling according to directions, adding 1 teaspoon vanilla, and pour over cream cheese layer. Chill until set. Garnish with whipped cream and toasted coconut. Makes 2 pies.

BIGHORN BANANA CREAM PIE

¾   cup sugar
⅓   cup flour
¼   teaspoon salt
2   cups milk
3   egg yolks, lightly beaten
2   tablespoons butter
1   teaspoon vanilla extract
1   pastry shell, baked
3   medium firm bananas
Whipping cream

In a saucepan, combine sugar, flour and salt; stir in milk and mix well. Cook over medium heat, stirring constantly, until mixture thickens and comes to a boil; boil for 2 minutes. Do not burn. Remove from heat. Stir a small amount into egg yolks; return all to saucepan. Cook for 2 minutes, stirring constantly. Remove from heat; add butter and vanilla. Cool slightly. Slice bananas into pastry shell; pour filling over. Cool. Before serving, garnish with whipped cream and a few banana slices. Serves: 6

LOWELL STRAWBERRY PIE

3   pints fresh strawberries
½   pint heavy cream
2   3-ounce packages cream cheese
½   cup sugar
3½ tablespoons lemon juice
1   9-inch pie shell, baked
½   cup currant or strawberry jelly

Wash and stem berries. Beat cream until stiff; cover and refrigerate. Beat together cream cheese, sugar and lemon juice until smooth and fluffy. Fold in whipped cream; cut in small berries, leave some for top decoration. Pile filling into pie shell. Place strawberries on top. Soften jelly, then spread over top of pie, glazing berries. Refrigerate or freeze. Also can use raspberries, blueberries, etc. Serves: 8

MACADAMIA RUM RAISIN ICE CREAM PIE

Crust:
12 ounces Oreo cookies
2   ounces whipped butter
Filling:
½   gallon rum raisin ice cream, softened
2   quarts Non-Dairy Topping, whipped
6   ounces raisins
1   ounce rum extract
1   pound macadamia nuts, chopped
6   ounces chocolate morsels

Mix ice cream on low speed; add topping, raisins, rum extract and nuts. Mix for 1 minute. Fold mixture into springform pan and level. Melt 6-ounces chocolate morsels and lace chocolate over top of pie in a crisscross motion.

USS ARIZONA PECAN PIE

1   cup white syrup
3   eggs
2   tablespoons butter, melted
½   cup brown sugar
½   cup white sugar
1   teaspoon vanilla
1   teaspoon vinegar
Dash salt
1   cup pecans

Beat eggs well, then add syrup, sugars and all ingredients. Mix well. Last add pecans and pour into uncooked pie shell. Bake at 350 degrees for 30 to 40 minutes.

KENNESAW PEACH COBBLER

2¼ cups flour
1 cup shortening
Salt
Peaches
1 cup sugar
2 tablespoons flour
Butter

Blend flour, shortening and a little salt. Add cold water to make dough stick together (several spoonfuls). Roll out in two parts. Put ½ on bottom of 9-inch square pan. Slice peaches in a large bowl; add sugar and 2 tablespoons flour. Pour peaches on dough and dot with lots of butter. Add a little water if peaches seem dry. Add top crust and prick with a fork or slit like a pie. Bake at 375 degrees for 45 minutes or until lightly brown. Serve with cream.

CAPITOL REEF PEACH CRISP

8 medium fresh peaches, peeled and sliced
1 cup flour
1 cup sugar
2 tablespoons brown sugar
¼ teaspoon salt
½ teaspoon cinnamon
½ cup butter or margarine, softened

Place peach slices in lightly greased 8-inch square baking dish. Set aside. Combine flour, sugar, brown sugar, salt and cinnamon in medium bowl, stirring well. Cut in butter with a pastry blender until mixture resembles coarse meal. Sprinkle flour mixture evenly over peaches. Bake at 375 degrees for 45 minutes or until crust is golden brown. Serves: 6-8

BLUEBERRY PANDOWDY

4 cups blueberries
⅔ cup sugar
2 tablespoons lemon juice
Whipped cream
Batter:
1½ cups flour
2 teaspoons baking powder
½ teaspoon salt
½ cup butter, softened
½ cup sugar
1 egg
½ cup milk

Combine berries, sugar and lemon juice in 9x9-inch pan. Mix together flour, baking powder and salt; set aside. Cream butter and sugar until fluffy. Add egg and beat until smooth. Add flour mixture alternately with milk and beat until smooth. Spread over berry mixture; bake 25 minutes at 375 degrees. Cut into squares and serve warm with whipped cream. Serves: 9

DINOSAUR BUTTER PECAN CRUNCH

2   cups graham cracker crumbs
½   cup butter or margarine, melted
2   3.4 ounce packages instant vanilla
    pudding mix
2   cups milk
1   quart butter pecan ice cream,
    softened slightly
1   8-ounce carton frozen whipped
    topping, thawed
2   1.4-ounces Heath candy bars,
    crushed

In a bowl, combine crumbs and butter. Pat into the bottom of an ungreased 13x9x2-inch pan. Chill. In a mixing bowl, beat pudding mixes and milk until well blended, about 1 minute. Fold in the ice cream and whipped topping. Spoon over crust. Sprinkle with crushed candy bars. Freeze. Thaw 20 minutes before serving. Serves: 12-16

GATEWAY ARCH APPLE CRISP

1   medium apple, peeled and sliced
1   tablespoon all-purpose flour
2   tablespoons brown sugar
1   tablespoon butter or margarine
2   tablespoons quick-cooking oats
⅛   teaspoon ground cinnamon
Cream, optional

Place apple slices in a small greased baking dish. In a small bowl, combine flour and brown sugar; cut in butter until mixture resembles coarse crumbs. Add oats and cinnamon. Sprinkle over apple slices. Bake, uncovered, at 350 degrees for 35-40 minutes or until tender. Serve with cream if desired. Serve: 1

ISLE ROYALE RICE PUDDING

¾   cup cooked white rice
3   large eggs, beaten
2   cups whole milk
1   cup evaporated milk
½   cup sugar
⅛   teaspoon salt
1¼ teaspoons vanilla extract
Ground cinnamon

Preheat oven to 350 degrees. Mix all ingredients except cinnamon in a large bowl until blended. Pour into an oblong baking dish and sprinkle generously with cinnamon. Bake 35 minutes. Serve hot or cold.

ADAMS BREAD PUDDING

½ loaf French bread
2 cups milk
3 eggs, slightly beaten
1 cup sugar
¼ cup margarine
1 tablespoon vanilla
2 teaspoons cinnamon

Tear bread into small pieces. Combine bread and milk in a large bowl, let stand 15 minutes, stirring often. Beat eggs, sugar, margarine, vanilla and cinnamon together. Stir into bread mixture. Turn into a greased 8x8x2-inch baking dish. Bake at 350 degrees for 40-45 minutes. Serve with Whiskey Sauce below.

WHISKEY SAUCE

¼ cup butter or margarine
½ cup sugar
1 egg yolk
2 tablespoons water
2 tablespoons bourbon

In a small saucepan melt butter. Stir in sugar, egg yolk and water. Cook, stirring constantly over medium-low heat 5 to 6 minutes, until sugar dissolves and thickens. Remove from heat; stir in bourbon. Spoon over warm bread pudding.

WHITE HOUSE DATE PUDDING

3 egg whites, beaten until stiff
1 cup sugar
1 cup pecans, chopped
1 8-ounce box dates, chopped
1 tablespoon baking powder

Mix all ingredients together and pour into medium-sized, greased baking dish. Bake 40 minutes at 325 degrees. This will have a crusty appearance. Serve with whipped cream.

RANGER HOT FUDGE PUDDING

½ cup flour, sifted
1 teaspoon baking powder
⅛ teaspoon salt
⅓ cup sugar
3 tablespoons cocoa
1 tablespoon butter, melted
¼ cup half and half
½ teaspoon vanilla
½ cup walnuts, chopped
½ cup brown sugar
¾ cup boiling water

Combine flour, baking powder, salt, sugar and 1 tablespoon cocoa; sift 3 times. Combine butter, cream and vanilla; add flour mixture and blend lightly. Stir in nuts. Pour into a buttered casserole. Combine brown sugar and remaining cocoa; sprinkle over batter. Pour boiling water gently over all. Bake at 350 degrees for 30 minutes. Serve warm with whipped cream.

Desserts

NATCHEZ TRACE CHERRY SQUARES

1   12-ounce angel food cake
1   cup whipping cream
1   8-ounce package cream cheese,
    softened
1   cup powdered sugar
1   20-ounce can cherry pie filling

Cut cake into 1-inch cubes. There should be about 8 cups. With electric mixer, beat whipping cream until soft peaks form. In a large bowl, beat cream cheese and powdered sugar until smooth. Stir in ¼ of whipped cream to lighten cheese. Fold in remaining whipped cream until thoroughly blended. Add cake cubes and fold until well mixed. Place in 7x11-inch dish; spread pie filling on top. Cut into squares after well chilled. Serve: 8

HARPERS FERRY CHOCOLATE PARFAITS

1   butter pound cake
1   package individual chocolate
    puddings
1   carton whipped topping
Pecans and whipped cream, optional

For each serving, place pound cake cube in bottom of parfait glass. Mix pudding with a little whipped topping and place on top of cake. Then a layer of whipped cream and pecans. Be creative!

BRIDALVEIL RASPBERRY SAUCE

1   12-ounce package frozen
    raspberries, thawed
½   cup sugar
2   tablespoons cornstarch

Combine raspberries, sugar and cornstarch; cook over low heat until thickened. Serve warm over cake or ice cream.

BOSTON ITALIAN CREAM CAKE

1 cup buttermilk
1 teaspoon baking soda
5 eggs, separated
2 cups sugar
1 teaspoon vanilla
1 3½-ounce can coconut
1 cup pecans, chopped
1 stick butter
½ cup shortening
2 cups flour
Icing:
1 8-ounce package cream cheese
1 teaspoon vanilla
1 stick butter
1 box powdered sugar, sifted

Combine soda and milk. Cream sugar, butter and shortening. Add egg yolks, one at a time; beat well. Add milk and flour alternately. Stir in vanilla. Beat egg whites until stiff; fold into mixture. Stir in nuts and coconut. Bake in three 9-inch greased and floured round cake pans for 30 minutes at 350 degrees.

ICING:
Cream the cheese with butter and add the powdered sugar a little at a time.

CHOCOLATE ITALIAN CREAM CAKE

½ cup butter
½ cup shortening
2 cups sugar
5 eggs, separated
2 cups flour
1 teaspoon baking soda
¼ cup cocoa
1 cup buttermilk
1 teaspoon vanilla extract
1 cup shredded coconut
½ cup pecans, chopped
Icing:
¼ cup butter
1 8-ounce package cream cheese
1 teaspoon vanilla
¼ cup cocoa
1 pound box powdered sugar
½ cup pecans
1 cup coconut

Cream butter, shortening and sugar together. Add egg yolks one at a time and beat well. Sift flour, baking soda and cocoa together. Add dry mixture to creamed mixture, alternating with buttermilk. Mix well. Stir in vanilla, coconut and pecans. Fold in beaten egg whites. Pour into three 9-inch round, greased and floured baking pans. Bake at 325 degrees for 25 minutes or until toothpick comes out clean. Remove from pans and cool on racks before icing. Assemble by icing between layers then top and sides of cake.
ICING:
Cream butter, cream cheese and vanilla together. Stir in cocoa and powdered sugar. Mix well. Add pecans and coconut and stir well.

CAPE HATTERAS CHOCOLATE CAKE

2   cups flour
2   cups sugar
½   teaspoon salt
2   eggs
1   cup water
3   tablespoons cocoa
½   cup oil
1   stick margarine
½   cup buttermilk
1   teaspoon soda
Icing:
1   box powdered sugar
1   stick margarine
2   tablespoons cocoa
3   to 4 tablespoons milk

Mix first 5 ingredients and set aside. Heat cocoa, oil and margarine and pour into flour mixture. Mix. Add buttermilk and soda. Pour into greased and floured oblong pan. Bake at 350 degrees for 30 minutes or until done.

*FOR ICING:*Mix all ingredients together and beat until smooth. Ice hot cake.

SOUR CREAM POUND CAKE

1   cup butter
2¾   cups sugar
6   eggs, separated
¼   teaspoon baking soda
½   teaspoon salt
3   cups flour, sifted before
     measuring
1   cup sour cream
1   teaspoon vanilla extract
1   teaspoon almond extract

Cream butter and sugar. Add egg yolks, one at a time. Add soda and salt to flour and sift 2 more times. Then add flour mixture and sour cream alternately to the butter and sugar mixture. Beat egg white until stiff and fold into batter. Bake in a greased and floured tube or Bundt pan at 350 degrees for 1¼ to 1½ hours or until toothpick comes out clean. When cool sprinkle with powdered sugar, if desired.

CUSTER'S ORANGE POUND CAKE

1   orange flavored cake mix
1   3¾-ounce package vanilla instant
     pudding
1   cup water
½   cup vegetable oil
4   eggs
1   cup powdered sugar, sifted
2   tablespoons orange juice

Heat oven to 350 degrees. Blend cake mix, pudding mix, water, oil and eggs in a large bowl; beat at medium speed for 2 minutes. Pour batter into a greased and floured 1-inch fluted pan. Bake 45 to 50 minutes, until center springs back when touched lightly. Cool 25 minutes in pan; invert onto serving plate. Combine powdered sugar and orange juice; add additional juice for desired consistency. Spoon over cake. Serves: 12-16

HIGH ALTITUDE CHOCOLATE CAKE

3	ounces unsweetened chocolate
½	cup plus 2 tablespoons shortening
1	cup sugar
1	cup brown sugar
4	eggs, separated
1	teaspoon baking soda
1½	cups milk or 1 cup buttermilk
3	cups cake flour, sifted
½	teaspoon salt
1	teaspoon vanilla

Preheat oven to 350 degrees. Grease and flour pans. Melt chocolate and let cool. Cream shortening and sugars. Then add egg yolks. Beat in chocolate. Dissolve soda in milk. Sift flour and salt together. Add dry ingredients with milk to chocolate mixture. Add vanilla last. Bake 30-35 minutes.

CHICKASAW PEACH CAKE

3	cups fresh peaches, sliced
3	tablespoons butter or margarine
1	cup flour
1½	teaspoons baking powder
3¼	cups sugar
1	cup boiling water
1	teaspoon almond extract
1	cup sugar
1	tablespoon cornstarch
½	teaspoon salt

Slice peaches into an 8x8-inch pan. Cream ¾ cup sugar and butter; add milk, almond extract, baking powder and flour; mix well. Pour over peaches. Combine 1 cup sugar, cornstarch and salt; sprinkle over batter. Pour boiling water over all and bake for 1 hour at 375 degrees.

WUPATKI APPLE CAKE SQUARES

1¼	cups Crisco oil
2	cups sugar
2	eggs
1	teaspoon salt
1	teaspoon baking soda
1	teaspoon cinnamon
2	teaspoons vanilla
3	cups flour, sifted
3	cups peeled and chopped apples

Mix all ingredients together in large bowl. Put in greased and floured 13x9-inch pan. Bake at 350 degrees for 55 minutes (will get quite brown). Cool. Glaze with powdered sugar and water glaze. Cut into squares. Stays very fresh.

PEA RIDGE POPPY SEED CAKE

1   package (2-layer size) yellow cake
    mix or pudding-included cake
    mix
1   package (4-serving size) Jell-O
    Brand instant pudding and pie
    filling
4   eggs
1   cup (½ pint) sour cream
¼   cup oil
½   cup cream sherry wine
¼   cup poppy seed
Orange Butter Glaze:
1½ tablespoons milk
1   tablespoon butter or margarine
1   tablespoon orange juice
1¼ cups confectioner's sugar
½   teaspoon orange rind, grated

Combine all ingredients in large mixer bowl. Blend, then beat at medium speed of electric mixer for 4 minutes. Pour into greased and floured 10-inch tube or fluted tube pan. Bake in preheated 350 degree oven for 50 minutes or until cake tester inserted in center comes out clean and cake begins to pull away from sides of pan. Do not overbake. Cool in pan 15 minutes. Remove from pan and finish cooling on rack. Spoon Orange Butter Glaze over cooled cake.

FOR GLAZE: heat milk, butter and orange juice in saucepan until butter is melted. Stir in confectioner's sugar and orange rind in a small bowl and beat until smooth. Makes ½ cup. Or sift powdered sugar over the cake. This is a super dessert, not too sweet.

MISSISSIPPI RIVER MUD CAKE

1   cup butter or margarine
2   cups granulated sugar
4   eggs
¼   cup cocoa powder
¾   teaspoon salt
1½ cups all-purpose flour
1   teaspoon vanilla extract
1½ cups flaked coconut
1½ cups chopped nuts (preferably
    pecans)
1   9-ounce jar marshmallow cream,
    or miniature marshmallows as
    needed
Frosting:
⅓   cup cocoa powder
½   cup butter or margarine
½   teaspoon vanilla extract
⅛   teaspoon salt
⅓   cup light cream or milk
1   16-ounce box confectioner's sugar

Cream butter and sugar in large mixing bowl. Beat eggs, one at a time. Sift cocoa, salt and flour, then add to egg mixture. Stir in vanilla, coconut and chopped nuts. Pour batter into a greased and floured 13x9x2-inch pan. Bake in a 350 degree oven for 30-35 minutes, or until toothpick inserted in center comes out clean. Remove from oven and, while hot, either spread with marshmallow cream or cover with miniature marshmallows and spread them after they have melted. Let cake cool, then frost with frosting.

FOR FROSTING: Beat cocoa, butter, vanilla, salt, cream and confectioner's sugar in a medium mixing bowl until fluffy. Spread over marshmallow cream on cake.

HORSESHOE BEND PUMPKIN RAISIN CAKE

2 cups all-purpose flour
2 cups sugar
2 teaspoons pumpkin pie spice
2 teaspoons baking powder
1 teaspoon baking soda
½ teaspoon salt
4 eggs
1 16-ounce can pumpkin
¾ cup vegetable oil
2 cups bran cereal (not flakes)
1 cup chopped pecans
1 cup raisins
Confectioners sugar, optional

Combine flour, sugar, pumpkin pie spice, baking powder, baking soda and salt; set aside. In a large bowl, beat eggs. Add pumpkin and oil; stir in cereal just until moistened. Add dry ingredients and stir just until combined. Fold in pecans and raisins. Pour into a greased 10-inch tube pan. Bake at 350 degrees for 60-65 minutes or until cake tests done. Cool in pan for 10 minutes before removing to a wire rack to cool completely. Dust with confectioners sugar before serving if desired. Serves: 12-16

CANYONLANDS ICE CREAM SAUCE

2 ounces unsweetened chocolate
1 tablespoon butter
½ cup boiling water
1 cup sugar
2 tablespoons light corn syrup
½ cup walnuts or toasted almonds
1 teaspoon vanilla
Dash salt

Melt chocolate and butter in double boiler; dilute with boiling water. Add sugar, salt and corn syrup; stir to dissolve sugar. Boil over direct heat 6 minutes, stirring often to prevent burning. Cool to room temperature. Add walnuts and vanilla. Serve over coffee ice cream.

VIRGIN ISLANDS STRAWBERRY YOGURT

2 cups strawberries, fresh or frozen
1 cup low-fat plain, unsweetened yogurt
⅓ cup powdered sugar (omit if using presweetened frozen strawberries)
1 tablespoon fresh lemon juice

In a food processor or blender, blend strawberries. Add the yogurt, powdered sugar and lemon juice; process until mixed (just a few seconds). Pour mixture into a 2-quart bowl or pan and freeze until barely firm (time will vary with different freezers). Next, beat the mixture with an electric mixer until smooth. Freeze again until firm. Remove from the freezer 15 to 30 minutes before serving, or until it is semi-soft. Makes five ½ cup servings.

SALEM MARITIME CHEESECAKE

Crust:
1   cup pecans, chopped
1   10-ounce box vanilla wafers
1   stick butter, softened

Mix all together and press into springform pan.

Filling:
4   eggs, beat whites stiff and set aside
3   8-ounce packages cream cheese
4   egg yolks, from above
1   cup sugar
1½ teaspoon vanilla
Sour Cream Mixture:
2   cups sour cream
½   cup sugar
1   teaspoon almond flavoring

Add beaten egg whites to combined creamed mixture. Pour creamed mixture in and bake at 350 degrees for 25 minutes. Remove from oven and set oven to 450 degrees. Spread sour cream mixture on top and bake for 10 minutes more. Leave in pan, cool and refrigerate. Make the day ahead. Top with pie filling or fruit glaze of your choice.

KINGS PALACE CHEESE CAKES

42 to 46 2-inch foil cups
1   box vanilla wafers
3   8-ounce packages cream cheese
⅔   cup sugar
3   eggs
1   teaspoon vanilla
Pie filling (cherry or blueberry)

Place one cookie, flat side up in each cup. Beat cream cheese, sugar, eggs and vanilla until smooth. Fill cups to about ¼-inch from top. Bake for 15 minutes at 350 degrees. Top with pie filling. Will make 42-46. These miniatures freeze well.

BACKCOUNTRY GRANOLA COOKIES

2   cups regular oats, uncooked
1   cup brown sugar, packed
1   cup butter, melted
2   eggs, beaten
¼   cup frozen orange juice concentrate, thawed
1   teaspoon baking soda
1½ cups flour
1   12-ounce package semisweet chocolate chips
1   cup raisins
1   cup unsalted dry roasted peanuts
1   teaspoon ground cinnamon
1   teaspoon vanilla
¼   teaspoon salt

Combine first 4 ingredients in a bowl; stir well. Combine orange juice concentrate and soda; add to oat mixture, stirring well. Add flour and remaining ingredients, stir to combine mix. Cover and chill one hour. Drop dough by tablespoon onto greased cookie sheet. Bake at 375 degrees for 10 minutes or until lightly browned.

BOSTON TEA SUGAR COOKIES

1   cup sugar, white
1   cup sugar, powdered
1   cup butter, soft
1   cup shortening
2   eggs
4½ cups flour
1   teaspoon baking soda
1   teaspoon cream of tartar
3   teaspoons vanilla

Combine and sift flour, soda and cream of tartar. Set aside. Cream butter, shortening and sugar. Beat well. Add eggs and continue to beat. Add flour mixture, then vanilla. Roll dough into small balls and place on ungreased cookie sheet. Press balls down with glass dipped in sugar. Bake at 375 degrees for 8-10 minutes.

BLUE RIDGE OATMEAL COOKIES

1   cup shortening
1   cup brown sugar
1   cup granulated sugar
2   eggs, beaten
2   tablespoons water
1½ cups flour
1   teaspoon soda
1   teaspoon salt
3   cups quick oats
½   cup nuts
1   teaspoon vanilla
1   cup dates, chopped

Cream shortening and sugars. Add eggs, water and vanilla. Then add sifted dry ingredients and mix well. Add oats, dates and nuts. Drop from teaspoon onto greased cookie sheet. Bake at 375 degrees 10 minutes.

CREAM CHEESE COOKIES

1   cup butter, softened
1   3-ounce package cream cheese, softened
1   cup sugar
1   egg yolk
2½ cups flour
1   teaspoon vanilla
Red candied cherries

Cream butter and cream cheese. Gradually add sugar, beating until light and fluffy. Add egg yolk, beating well. Add flour and vanilla. Mix until blended. Chill dough at least one hour. Shape dough into 1-inch balls and place on greased cookie sheet. Press a candied cherry into each cookie. Bake at 325 degrees for 12-15 minutes.

Desserts

GREAT SMOKIES OATMEAL COOKIES

1 cup flour, sifted
½ cup sugar
½ teaspoon baking powder
½ teaspoon baking soda
¼ teaspoon salt
½ cup brown sugar
½ cup shortening
1 egg
¼ teaspoon vanilla
¾ cup quick oats
¼ cup nuts, chopped

Sift flour, white sugar, baking powder, soda and salt. Add brown sugar, shortening, egg and vanilla. Beat well. Stir in oats and nuts. Form into small balls and dip tops in a little sugar. Bake on ungreased cookie sheet at 375 degrees for 10 minutes.

BUFFALO RIVER CHIPS

4 sticks butter, melted
2 cups light brown sugar, packed
2 cups white sugar
4 eggs
2 teaspoons vanilla
2 cups quick oats
2 cups cornflakes
4 cups flour
2 teaspoons baking powder
2 teaspoons baking soda
1 teaspoon salt
1 6-ounce package chocolate chips
2 cups coarsley chopped pecans

Mix butter, brown sugar and white sugar together. Stir in eggs, vanilla, oats and cornflakes. Sift together flour, baking powder, soda and salt and add to butter and sugar mixture. Mix well. Stir in chocolate chips and pecans. Use ice cream scoop to drop on cookie sheet (6 cookies per sheet). Bake at 350 degrees for about 16 minutes.

KLONDIKE COOKIES

1 cup shortening
1 cup sugar
1 cup brown sugar, packed
2 eggs
1 teaspoon vanilla extract
1½ cups flour
1 teaspoon salt
2 cups regular oats, uncooked
2 cups pecans, chopped
1 cup crisp rice cereal
1 cup flaked coconut

Cream shortening; gradually add sugars, beating well with electric mixer. Add eggs and vanilla, beating well. Combine flour and salt; add to creamed mixture, mixing well. Stir in oats and remaining ingredients. Drop dough by heaping tablespoonfuls onto greased cookie sheet. Bake at 325 degrees for 10-12 minutes. Cool slightly on cookie sheets. Remove to wire racks to cool.
Yield: 6 dozen

FORT MCHENRY DREAM BARS

Crust:
½ cup shortening or butter
½ cup brown sugar
1 cup flour
½ teaspoon salt

Filling:
1 cup brown sugar
1 teaspoon vanilla
2 eggs, beaten
2 tablespoons flour
½ teaspoon baking powder
1½ cups shredded coconut
½ cup pecans, chopped

Cream shortening and sugar. Add flour and salt. Blend. Spread in 8x12-inch pan. Bake at 350 degrees for 15 minutes; cool. Mix vanilla and sugar with beaten eggs. Add flour and baking powder. Blend well. Mix in coconut and pecans. Spread on first layer. Bake 20 minutes at 325 degrees. Makes 24 bars.

COLONIAL COCONUT COOKIES

3½ cups flour
1 egg, beaten
1 cup sugar
½ cup sweet milk
1 teaspoon vanilla
¾ cup butter
3 teaspoons baking powder
2 cups chopped nuts
2 cans coconut

Cream butter and sugar. Add egg which has been beaten. Sift baking powder and flour; add flour alternately with sweet milk. Add nuts, coconut and vanilla. Drop from spoon on baking sheet. Bake 350 degrees for approximately 15 minutes or until done.

GRAND PORTAGE CREAM CHEESE BROWNIES

1 4-ounce package sweet cooking chocolate
2 tablespoons butter or margarine
3 eggs
1½ teaspoons vanilla
1 cup sugar
½ cup all-purpose flour
½ teaspoon baking powder
¼ teaspoon salt
½ cup chopped walnuts
1 3-ounce package cream cheese, softened

Melt chocolate and butter; cool. In bowl beat together 2 eggs and 1 teaspoon vanilla; gradually add ¾ cup sugar. Continue beating until thick and lemon colored. Stir together flour, baking powder, and ¼ teaspoon salt; add to egg mixture. Beat well. Blend in chocolate mixture and nuts; set aide. Cream together cream cheese and ¼ cup sugar until fluffy. Blend in remaining egg and vanilla. Spread half of the chocolate mixture in a greased and floured 8x8x2-inch baking pan. Pour cheese mixture over; top with remaining chocolate mixture. Swirl layers to marble. Bake at 350 degrees 40-45 minutes. Cool. Cut into squares. Makes 16.

PETERSBURG LEMON COOKIES

1   cup cake flour, sifted
2   tablespoons sugar
⅛   teaspoon salt
⅓   cup butter or margarine, softened
2   eggs, slightly beaten
1   cup brown sugar, firmly packed
½   cup chopped pecans
½   cup grated coconut
½   teaspoon vanilla
Lemon Glaze:
⅔   cup powdered sugar, sifted
1   tablespoon lemon juice
1   teaspoon lemon rind, grated

Sift flour, sugar and salt into a bowl. Cut in butter until mixture resembles coarse meal. Press firmly over the bottom of greased 9-inch square pan. Bake at 350 degrees for 15 minutes or until pastry is lightly browned. Meanwhile, mix eggs, brown sugar, nuts, coconut and vanilla. Pour over partially baked pastry. Bake 30 minutes or until topping is firm. Cool 15 minutes. FOR LEMON GLAZE: Blend powdered sugar, lemon juice and lemon rind together until smooth. Spread on top of cookies. Cut in 32 small bars. Cool.

EDISON SUGAR AND SPICE COOKIES

¾   cup Crisco
1   cup sugar
1   egg
¼   cup molasses
2   cups flour
2   teaspoons soda
¼   teaspoon salt
1   teaspoon cinnamon
¾   teaspoon cloves
¾   teaspoon ginger

Mix thoroughly; form into balls the size of walnuts. Place on greased cookie sheet. Bake at 375 degrees for 10-12 minutes. Roll in powdered sugar while still warm. Makes 4 to 5 dozen cookies.

WHISKEYTOWN BROWNIE COOKIE

⅔   cup shortening
1½ cups brown sugar, packed
1   tablespoon water
1   teaspoon vanilla extract
2   eggs
1½ cups all-purpose flour
⅓   cup baking cocoa
½   teaspoon salt
¼   teaspoon baking soda
2   cups (12-ounces) semisweet
    chocolate chips
½   cup chopped walnuts or pecans
    (optional)

In a large mixing bowl, cream shortening, sugar, water and vanilla. Beat in eggs. Combine flour, cocoa, salt and baking soda; gradually add to creamed mixture and beat just until blended. Stir in chocolate chips and nuts if desired. Drop rounded teaspoonfuls 2-inches apart on ungreased baking sheet. Bake at 375 degrees for 7-9 minutes; do not overbake. Cool 2 minutes before removing to wire racks. Yield: 3 dozen

WILD PLUM JELLY

5	pounds wild plums, halved and pitted
4	cups water
1	1¾-ounce package powdered fruit pectin
7½	cups water

In a large kettle, simmer plums and water until tender, about 30 minutes. Pour through a damp jelly bag, allowing juice to drip into a bowl. Measure 5½ cups of juice; return to the kettle. Add pectin; stir and bring to a boil. Add sugar; bring to a full rolling boil. Boil for 1 minute, stirring constantly. Remove from the heat; skim off any foam. Pour hot into jars, leaving ¼-inch headspace. Adjust caps. Process for 5 minutes in a boiling-water bath. Yield: about 8 half-pints

STRAWBERRY DIET JAM

¾	cup diet lemon-lime soda
1	3-ounce package sugar free strawberry gelatin
1	cup strawberries, mashed
1½	teaspoons lemon juice

In a saucepan, bring soda to a boil. Remove from heat and stir in gelatin until dissolved. Stir in strawberries and lemon juice. Pour into jars, cover and refrigerate up to 3 weeks. Do not freeze. Yield: 1¾ cups

PICTURED ROCKS HOUSE AROMA

32	ounces apple juice
46	ounces pineapple juice
2	cups water
2	sticks cinnamon
1	tablespoon whole cloves
1	tablespoon whole allspice
1	teaspoon ground ginger

Mix all ingredients together and simmer. This gives off a fragrant aroma that is delightful and deodorizes the house. Add more liquid, either juice or water from time to time when mixture cooks down. Store in a covered plastic container and keep in the freezer or fridge when not in use. It lasts and lasts.

THE JEFFERSON NATIONAL EXPANSION MEMORIAL

The City of St. Louis lies on the west bank of the Mississippi River in Missouri. In 1764 French fur traders built a post on this inland site. The Indians supplying furs to the traders could easily reach the spot via canoe.

The settlement came under United States control when President Thomas Jefferson bought the Louisiana Territory from France in 1803. During the 1800's St. Louis became the "Gateway to the West." The city was busy with steamboat travel and became a major railroad center after the Civil War. The rail depot is one of the most beautiful in the country. During the late 1800's St. Louis became a major urban center.

The Jefferson National Expansion Memorial, honoring Thomas Jefferson and the pioneers who settled the West, majestically stands on the St. Louis riverfront. Truly a monumental piece of work, Eero Saarinen's stainless steel gateway arch stands 630 feet high, making it the nation's tallest monument.

Also interesting are the Old Courthouse where the famous Dred Scott sued for freedom, the museum and Old Cathedral. If you love history, this park needs to be on your list to visit.

JEFFERSON NATIONAL EXPANSION MEMORIAL

The *U.S.S. Arizona Memorial*, HI is a floating memorial marking the spot where the U.S.S. Arizona was sunk in Pearl Harbor December 7, 1941 during the Japanese attack.

General George Washington's headquarters at *Valley Forge National Historical Park*, PA was the site of the Continental Army's winter encampment in 1777-1778.

A visit to the palatial *Vanderbilt Mansion National Historical Site*, NY shows visitors the lifestyles of the 19th century rich Americans.

Vicksburg National Military Park, MS boasts reconstructed forts and trenches to commemorate the 47 day siege on the city in 1863. The National Cemetery and its many state monuments leave visitors with powerful patriotic feelings.

The *Vietnam Veterans Memorial*, Washington, D.C., is a somber impressive black granite wall dedicated to those who lost their lives or are missing in Viet Nam.

Everyone loves the quiet coves, blue green waters and wonderful beaches of the *Virgin Islands National Park*, VI.

Voyageurs National Park, MN is named for the voyageurs, French Canadians who paddled birch-bark canoes for fur trading companies in the late 1700's and early 1800's.

The three units of *Whiskeytown-Shasta-Trinity National Recreation Area*, CA are managed by the U.S. Forest Service and the National Park Service. Whiskeytown, managed by the National Park Service, informs visitors about the California Gold Rush Days. Whiskeytown Lake is a great boating and sailing lake.

The sparkling white sand dunes of *White Sands National Monument*, NM rise to sixty feet heights and cover 275 square miles. Visitors are in awe of this largest gypsum dunefield in the world.

Wind Cave National Park, SD is a limestone cave in the Black Hills of South Dakota decorated by beautiful boxwork, a pattern of thin fins of calcite on the walls and ceilings. The park also has a large buffalo herd.

The Filene Center at *Wolf Trap Farm Park* for the Performing Arts, VA is an open air performing arts pavilion outside Washington, D.C., which attracts performers from around the world.

Wilbur and Orville Wright made their first flight in 1903 at *Wright Brothers National Monument*, NC. What then seemed a nearly impossible task has turned out to be a common way of travel today.

Zion National Park, UT is full of beautiful scenery with canyons, mesas, and former volcanic activity. The park was established November 19, 1919.

Camping & Picnics

CAMPGROUND EGGS

4   eggs
4   squares heavy foil each 7x7-inches

For each serving, make a foil cup by molding a 7-inch square of heavy foil around bottom of a 16-ounce fruit or vegetable can; remove can. Crack an egg into each cup. Place cups on grill over medium-low coals and cook 10 minutes or until desired doneness.

APPLE RAISIN PANCAKES

1   14-ounce package apple-cinnamon muffin mix
2   eggs
⅔   cup water
2   tablespoons cooking oil
½   cup raisins

In bowl, combine muffin mix, eggs and water; beat until smooth. Stir in cooking oil and raisins. Using 2 table-spoons batter for each. Cook pancakes over low heat on lightly oiled griddle. Makes two dozen 2½-inch pancakes.

PANCAKE MIX VARIATIONS

2   cups complete pancake mix
1⅓ cups water
1   cup ham, finely chopped or 1 cup blueberries or 1 8-ounce can whole kernel corn, drained

Combine pancake mix, water and ham. Using 2 tablespoons batter for each, cook pancakes over low heat on oiled griddle. Makes 18 small pancakes.

COLORADO HOT CHOCOLATE

Make the dry mixture at home and bring along in a plastic bag.
1   cup sugar
¾   cup cocoa powder
3   cups nonfat dry milk powder
Dash salt
8   cups water

Combine sugar and cocoa powder; add milk powder and salt. Place in saucepan. Add 1 cup of the water and stir until combined. Stir in remaining water and heat through (don't boil). Makes 8 servings.

FOR 1 SERVING: Place ⅓ cup dry mixture in cup. Stir in about 2 table-spoons cold water; mix well. Pour in enough boiling water to fill cup and stir.

LBJ BISCUITS 'N GRAVY

1   package canned biscuits
¾   cup flour
3   cups milk
Sausage or hamburger meat drippings

In a skillet, add flour to meat drippings to make a paste. Add milk and stir. Let gravy simmer a bit and add cooked sausage or hamburger to mixture. Pour over cooked biscuits.

GRAND CANYON CHILI

1   pound ground beef
1   onion, diced
1   can tomatoes
1   can chili beans
1   small can tomato sauce
1   tablespoon chili powder
Salt

Brown ground beef and onion in skillet. Drain excess fat. Add all ingredients and simmer for 30 minutes.

VALLEY FORGE STEW

1   pound ground beef
1   medium onion, chopped
1   can beef consomme
1   pound can cream style corn
1   pound can lima beans
3   large potatoes, diced
1   small can carrots

Brown beef and onion. Add consomme, potatoes, salt and pepper. Mix; cover and cook over low heat for 30 minutes. Add vegetables. Heat thoroughly.

CAPITOL REEF BEANS

1	large onion
2	pounds ground beef
1	can pinto beans
1	can Rotel tomatoes
1	teaspoon mustard
1	cup ketchup
1	can pork and beans
1	can lima beans
1	cup barbecue sauce
½	cup brown sugar

Cook onion and ground beef in skillet. Drain grease off meat and combine all ingredients in pot. Simmer for 45 minutes.

STREAM TO SKILLET FISH

Fried

Flour fish and place in buttered skillet. Cook until tender.

Baked

Flour fish and place in buttered skillet. Add small amount of water, tomato juice or milk. Cover with lid and place on hot coals.

Steamed

Wrap fish in foil; salt and pepper. Seal edges and place in coals for 10 minutes per side.

CAPE LOOKOUT HAMBURGERS

2	pounds ground beef
1	onion, chopped
1	tablespoon A-1 sauce
Grated Cheddar cheese	
Salt and pepper to taste	

Salt and pepper beef. Add onion and A-1 sauce. Mix well. Make 12 thin patties. Put some cheese on 6 patties. Top with the other 6 patties. Press edges together. Grill or freeze for later use.

JEFFERSON SKILLET SPAGHETTI

1   **pound ground beef**
1   **16-ounce can spaghetti sauce with mushrooms**
1¾ **cups water**
4   **ounces spaghetti, broken**

In skillet over medium coals, brown ground beef; drain off excess fat. Add spaghetti sauce and water. Bring to boiling: add broken spaghetti, stirring to separate strands. Simmer, covered, for 25-30 minutes or until spaghetti is tender, stirring frequently. Serve with Parmesan cheese, if desired. Serves: 4

SAN ANTONIO CHILI DOGS

8   **frankfurters**
8   **frankfurter buns, buttered**
1   **15-ounce can chili with beans**
1   **cup crushed corn chips**

Make a lengthwise slit in each frank; place one in each bun. Open slit. Stir together chili and corn chips; spoon onto slit franks in buns. Wrap each bun in foil; twist end to seal. Bake in 400 degree oven for 20 minutes. Serve with catsup, if desired. Serves: 8

CHANNEL ISLANDS POTATOES

4   **large potatoes, sliced thin**
1   **large onion, sliced thin**
½   **can green chile, chopped**
½   **green pepper, diced**
¼   **cup oil**
Salt and pepper to taste

Heat oil in skillet; add potatoes, green pepper and onion. Fry until tender. Add green chile, salt and pepper.

C & O PORK 'N BEANS

1	large can pork and beans
½	green pepper
½	pound bacon
½	large onion, chopped
½	cup catsup
½	cup brown sugar

Brown bacon and onion. Add all ingredients and simmer over coals for one hour. Add cut hot dogs for complete meal.

CAMPFIRE POTATOES

Baked

Wrap potatoes in foil. Place in coals for one hour.

Boiled

Peel potatoes, cut up and place in pan of water. Boil for 45 minutes until tender.

Fried

Peel and dice finely. Add chopped onion for variety. Salt and pepper. Place in skillet with 2 tablespoons oil for 15 minutes. Can also use canned potatoes.

EISENHOWER GREEN BEANS

2 cans French cut green beans, drained
1 can cream of mushroom soup
½ can milk or water
2 tablespoons onion flakes
Almonds, if desired

Place all ingredients in pan. Place in coals until hot.

STEAMTOWN CINNAMON DROPS

*Another time, snip refrigerated biscuits
into quarters, roll in cinnamon-sugar
and bake until lightly browned.*
2   cups packaged biscuit mix
⅔   cup water
¼   cup sugar
1   teaspoon ground cinnamon

Mix biscuit mix, water and half of the sugar until blended. Drop dough from teaspoon into mixture of remaining sugar and the cinnamon. Roll each ball to coat entire surface. Place on baking sheet or greased sheet of heavy foil. Bake in 350 degree oven for 10-12 minutes or until golden. Makes 24 rolls.

APPALACHIAN TRAIL MIX

1   package of sugared cereal
2   cups M & M's candy
2   cups salted nuts
2   cups raisins

Combine all ingredients and pack in individual plastic bags.

SAN FRANCISCO ENERGY BARS

2   tablespoons butter or margarine
2   cups tiny marshmallows or 20
     large marshmallows, snipped
2   tablespoons peanut butter
4   cups high protein cereal
Optional:
½   cup semisweet chocolate pieces

In saucepan, melt butter or margarine. Add marshmallows; heat and stir until melted and mixture is syrupy. Remove from heat; stir in peanut butter. Add cereal(and chocolate pieces if desired) and mix until coated. Press into an 8x8x2-inch square on a sheet of heavy foil. Cool until firm enough to cut into 2x1-inch bars. Makes 32 bars.

BLUEBERRY MUFFIN BREAD

2   9-inch foil pie pans
1   package blueberry muffin mix
Spring-type clothespins
Butter or margarine

Lightly grease the foil pans. Prepare muffin mix according to package directions; pour into one of the pans. Cover with second pan, inverted. Secure rims together with clothespins. Place on grill over low coals. Cook 15 minutes on each side, rotating pan occasionally for even baking. Remove top pan; cut bread into 6 wedges. Serve with butter or margarine. Serves: 6

SAGAMORE HILL S'MORES

2   marshmallows
2   graham cracker squares
1   chocolate square

In order place chocolate on cracker, then toasted marshmallow and top with cracker.

WASHINGTON APPLES

4   apples
Filling:
Brown sugar
Cinnamon
Dab of butter
Nuts
Raisins

Core apple and peel about ⅓ down. Place filling in center. Wrap each apple in foil and seal edges. Place in dutch oven for 45 minutes.

RECIPE INDEX

RECIPE INDEX

RECIPE INDEX

PARK INDEX

PARK INDEX